GHOSTS AND WITCHES
OF THE COTSWOLDS

GHOSTS
and witches of the
COTSWOLDS

by J. A. BROOKS

Jarrold Publishing, Norwich

ISBN 0–7117–0233–0
© *Jarrold Publishing 1986*
Published by Jarrold Publishing, Norwich
First published 1986
Reprinted 1990
Printed in Great Britain. 3/90

Contents

Death and the Gentleman.

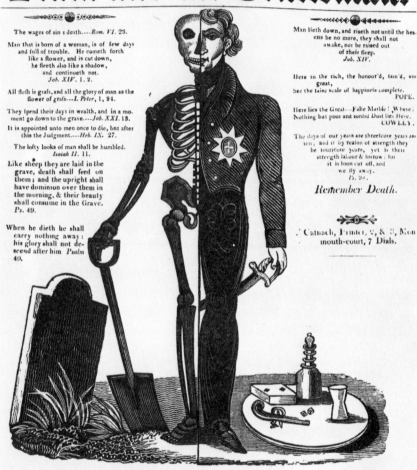

The wages of sin is death....*Rom. VI.* 23.

Man that is born of a woman, is of few days
and full of trouble. He cometh forth
like a flower, and is cut down,
he fleeth also like a shadow,
and continueth not.
Job. XIV. 1. 2.

All flesh is grafs, and all the glory of man as the
flower of grafs---*I. Peter*, 1, 24.

They spend their days in wealth, and in a moment go down to the grave.----*Job. XXI.* 13.

It is appointed unto men once to die, but after
this the Judgment.----*Heb. IX.* 27.

The lofty looks of man shall be humbled.
Isaiah II. 11.

Like sheep they are laid in the
grave, death shall feed on
them; and the upright shall
have dominion over them in
the morning, & their beauty
shall consume in the Grave.
Ps. 49.

When he dieth he shall
carry nothing away:
his glory shall not de-
scend after him *Psalm*
49.

Man lieth down, and riseth not until the hea-
ens be no more, they shall not
awake, nor be raised out
of their sleep.
Job. XIV.

Here in the rich, the honour'd, fam'd, and
great,
See the false scale of happinefs complete.
POPE.

Here lies the Great---False Marble! Where
Nothing but poor and sordid Dust lies Here.
COWLEY.

The days of our years are threescore years and
ten; and if by reason of strength they
be fourscore years, yet is their
strength labour & forrow: for
it is soon cut off, and
we fly away.
Ps. 90.

Remember Death.

Catnach, Printer, 2, & 3, Mon
mouth-court, 7 Dials.

THOU wealthy man of large possessions here
some thousand pounds a year,
ppression, from the poor,
me that thou shalt be no more.
efore in order set with speed,
nd how you your life doth lead

I strike the man, perhaps in dead of night,
Who hardly lives to see the morning light.
I am sent each hour, like to a nimble page,
To infants, hoary head, and middle age,
Time after time I sweep the world quite through,
Then 'tis in vain to think I'll favour you.(I bear,
R.MAN. Proud Death! you'll see what awful sway

Something to say that he might sta
Yet if ten thousand arguments the
The destiny of dying to excuse,
They'll find it is in vain with me to
'Tis I that part the dearest friends
Poor parents die, and leave their c
With nothing to support them here
But the kind hand of gracious Prov
Who is their father, friend, and sol

Foreword

This book embraces a wide field and must serve as an anthology rather than as any kind of a definitive work. Witchcraft and ghosts are not necessarily allied subjects though in many areas they share common ground.

The reader may find some elements of the stories repetitious. In most cases it would seem that if a fireside story-teller found a good plot then he stole it and elaborated his own version of the village ghost around it. This is not to say that the incident on which the story is based did not occur, however.

There are many tales here, found in local libraries, that seem to have escaped scrutiny for a generation or more, but there is also a marked lack of modern stories with any basis in fact. Should any reader have had a supernatural experience that he or she thinks worth relating the publisher would be glad to hear from him or her so that it may be included in a future edition.

The staff of the Reference and Local History sections in the Public Libraries at Birmingham, Cheltenham, Gloucester, Oxford, and Stratford-upon-Avon were most helpful, and without them this book could never have been written.

The Seven Whistlers

The Seven Whistlers
(An Old Worcestershire Delusion)

Seven spirits are there, from the underworld
Sent by the prescient dead
To warn men against ill: they fly by night
Like winged phantoms, and fill hearts with fright
When they pass over head.

These beings mystical, these forms of air,
These rangers of heaven's road,
Unseen in the thick darkness come and go
With ominous and awesome notes of woe,
Disaster to forbode.

They wing their way by two, by four, by six –
Though seven the dead may send;
Some call them the Seven Whistlers! – not a bird
Flies faster, but no man the seventh hath heard –
His croak means the world's end.

Weird is their whistling, like to whispers hoarse –
As if a corpse should call:
When two of them make utterance in the night,
Look for the lightning, and the tempest's might,
By which great harm may fall.

If four of the Seven Whistlers make their moan
From the dark ways on high,
Prepare for awful happenings; dire distress,
Murrain and famine, death and wretchedness,
And pray they pass thee by.

And when, of the night-fliers, six sound forth
Their warnings through the air,
Fear the swift earthquake and regard thy life;
Or wait war's havock, with red ruin rife,
And misery few may bear.

But should the Seven Whistlers whoop at once
Then shall earth's fate impend;
Some starry sphere, displaced may be, shall dash
The world to fragments in a shattering crash,
And all things have an end.

JOHN COTTON

10

This singular old legendary superstition of the 'Seven Whistlers' – which I have freely interpreted in the foregoing verses – had some local currency when I was a boy upwards of fifty years ago; though I think it prevailed more in the southern part of the county than in the northern. Many old country people then used to listen for and regard as omens of a supernatural character such sounds as, coming from the sky at night, they could not ascribe to owls or birds they were familiar with. I have known people pause in the dark, and after intently listening in a serious way, observe 'Ah, I thought I heard the Whistlers!' and seem much relieved that they had not. The Owl and Raven, as well as various other birds on occasion, have always been regarded as unlucky, and Swan sounds sometimes betokened death. Spencer, the poet, refers to 'The Whistler shrill, that whoso heares doth die'. If my memory serves me aright, the 'Seven Whistlers' were also locally known as the 'Night-flyers.' It is most probable that the sounds made by the whirring wings and low melancholy calls of birds of passage flying overhead in the night time gave rise to this superstition of the Seven Whistlers, the sounds made by the unseen birds being regarded by the credulous as the warning calls or intimations of spirits. Seven, too, was a sacred number. The belief is of very ancient, probably Celtic origin; for the Irish have many folk beliefs as to voices in the winds. There are also German and other legends as to Mythical Swans, &c. The calls of the Seven Whistlers, or Night Flyers, were very variously interpreted by those who heard them. Country people, having little to do with the world at large, generally attributed to them a local purport, such as the foretelling of serious accidents, or the death of a member of the hearer's family, of a horse or other animal, or of some calamity to the parish: they seldom gave the sounds wider significance. No one had ever heard all the Seven Whistlers *at once*; when this did happen it was supposed that a disaster beyond conception would occur.

In connection with this Midland belief in winged spirits, like birds, there is the story of the fluttering bird that came to the window of Thomas Lord Littleton (1779) three nights before he died, and which was looked upon as a messenger to warn him of his coming end. There is also a singular story told in Walpole's

(Lord Orford's) letters, about a Worcester lady who, believing that her dead daughter yet existed and might communicate with her as a singing bird, had cages of birds put with her in her pew in the cathedral. This the authorities are said to have allowed because the lady, though very eccentric, as might be supposed, was rich and pious, and had been a considerable benefactress to the cathedral.

The poem, and explanation also by John Cotton, is reprinted verbatim *from the* Bromsgrove Messenger *of 27 March 1909.*

The Midnight Hags

The Midnight Hags

On 24 January 1836, Bevil Blizard died at Oxenton. He was then said to be the 'last Necromancer of Winchcombe' though this claim may very well be wildly inaccurate for magic and witchcraft survived in other parts of the Cotswolds well into this century, and there is evidence that the number of active covens is on the increase today. Bevil, it was said, had supernatural powers bestowed on him by the Evil One. Even after his death at the great age of ninety-four his spirit was unable to rest and he was frequently seen by villagers, usually at the church gates.

Many strange stories are told of him. Once, when cutting hay in the fields, he announced to his work-mates that his hen-roost was being robbed, and left them in a hurry. To their amazement his scythe carried on working without him. Another of his powers was the ability to seek out thieves. Anthony Martin stole a scythe (a particularly despicable crime this, in a rural area where the implement was a prized possession, for over the years a man's body grew into its shape so that it could take ages to get used to a new one). The victim paid for a consultation with Blizard who gave him his own scythe and sharpened it for a halfpenny. It proved to be a wonderful tool, far better than the one that had been stolen. Blizard told the labourers that Martin was the culprit but that the theft would do him little good. Nor did it for his joints froze up.

Bevil was exceptional in that he was a male witch (Blizard the Wizard, in fact) but not unique (see the story of the Worcester-shire Wizard below). The majority of witches were, of course, women, and generally old ones at that, as in fairytales. They possessed a multitude of powers – they could cause you to fall sick with a strange, sometimes fatal, illness. They could prevent your milk from turning to butter in the churn, turn themselves into the shape of animals to travel about the countryside or escape

14

from pursuers, or charm away many of the common ills.

There are three categories of witches: white ones befriend man and help him in any way possible; grey ones use magic for their own purposes but are not actively good or bad; while black witches compact with the Devil to bring evil into all things. Satan has to make a formal contract with his witches who, for their part, have to surrender soul and body to him and sign a deed stating this with their own blood. The Devil, disguised as a man in black, gives a coin in receipt for this which signifies the completed sale. The new witch then has a familiar spirit given her, often a black cat, which helps her in her wicked ways and draws her blood for nourishment.

One of the witches of Long Compton would, or could, only assume the form of a white animal – sometimes a rabbit, a cat, or even a mouse. It was while she was in the guise of a white rabbit that she was run over and appeared the next day with a bandaged arm. As J. Harvey Bloom remarks in *Folk Lore, Old Customs and Superstitions in Shakespeare's Land* (London, 1929, a valuable source book), who can gainsay such evidence, especially since werewolves as well as Cinderella suffer from the same disadvantage?

In November, 1892, the *Winchcombe Record* reported another case of transmogrification. Ady Webb was an old woman living at Broadwater Cottage. A hare, being chased, jumped in the window of her cottage, injuring itself in the process. When the huntsmen entered there was Ady sitting by her fire, blood running from arm. On another occasion she was refused a drink by a carter; immediately afterwards his load of hay slipped off the wagon.

Some of the spells cast had alarming effects on those close to the victim. Another story from Long Compton tells of 'Old Mrs H. . . . who was so badly bewitched that she could not die while her relatives were present, so at her entreaty both they and her neighbours left the room. At once there arose a terrible tumult; on rushing in they found her possessions strewn about and her boxes and chests of drawers turned inside out in dire confusion. A black pigeon flew out of the window – the old lady was dead.' (J. Harvey Bloom.) It used to be said of this place that there were enough witches in the village to draw a wagon-load of hay

15

up Long Compton hill. Salford is a neighbouring village, lying on the far side of the Rollright Stones. A witch named Dolly Henderson lived in the village in the 1850s. She quarrelled with a neighbour, and bewitched her so that she fell seriously ill with a wasting disease. In dire straits she sought out a 'cunning man' named Manning. He told her that he would help if she could keep a secret, which was that she would meet with the woman who had cast the spell on her way home. She was not to speak to her or tell anyone of her sorcery. Poor Ann was a gossip, however, and after meeting with Dolly Henderson fell in with a group of women and told them all about her misfortunes. Subsequently her health failed even further until she looked like a skeleton. By a strange chance she met with a boy who was also suffering from one of Dolly's curses. Both were released from the evil magic when the boy's brother threw a thorn-stick at the old witch and scratched her arm. The magic was transferred to the witch who herself went into decline and soon died 'and the terror of the village was got rid of'. This tale was told in 1897 by a Mrs Jenny Bigerstaffe and shows how seriously witchcraft was taken even comparatively recently.

In 1875 James Heywood killed an old lady named Ann Turner (or Tennant) with a pitchfork at Long Compton. He claimed to be a latter-day witch-hunter and said that Ann Turner was one of sixteen witches living in the village. By killing her and spilling her blood he was able to undo the spells she had cast. His trial triggered off hysteria against witches in the Vale of the Red Horse so that hardly any old lady felt safe. In court the crazed young man asked that the body of his victim should be weighed against the church bible, a rare reference to a bizarre ancient custom. Heywood was convicted of manslaughter and imprisoned for life, but the incident may well have been remembered and used as the pattern for a murder which took place at Lower Quinton seventy years later (see below).

In the library at Stratford-upon-Avon there is an unpublished manuscript by J. Harvey Bloom which gives more details of the methods used against witches. This is a story about witchcraft at Wolford:

About 50 years since a witch and wizard named Grace Pain

and her husband were a source of alarm and terror here.
Grace bewitched her own son and it was commonly said
Sir Peter Poole could not rest in the place because of her.
My informant, Mrs Salmon, tells me Grace bewitched her

A labourer's cottage in the Cotswolds c. 1790

brother so that he barked like a dog and rode on chairs about the room till the sweat rolled off him; he was quiet when she was present but terrible when she left. Eric Pain, the husband, used to bewitch horses, thus a team drawing a load of hay would remain endeavouring to draw it till the foam and sweat covered them, but in spite of the whip could make no progress until he spoke, when the hay-load was drawn with no difficulty. Grace herself frequently ran about in the form of a hare, and at one time there was talk of weighing her against the Church Bible. This she strongly resented. (18 January, 1905.)

Later Bloom tells of drawing blood from a witch at Tysoe:

Not many years ago some people arrived from Brailes for the purpose of drawing blood from Agnes Durham, a reputed witch. While one engaged her in conversation, another got behind her, and suddenly seizing her hand, cruelly scored the back of it with a large corking pin.

Possibly Agnes was fortunate in escaping the more drastic and permanent remedy practised on Ann Turner against the Evil Eye, yet there is no wonder that old ladies lived in constant dread of being thought witches. Bloom mentions this too:

I have always considered that the unwillingness of old village women to use the support of a walking-stick in their old age is that all witches use walking-sticks. – An old woman named Ann Walker, who walked with a stick, was looked upon as a witch. A few years ago strange whirring noises were heard every night in her house. Crowds used to go to hear them, but the cause was never discovered. People from Radway came over to listen and vowed that her cottage was carried to the top of Edge Hill every night and came back in the morning. A stonemason who lived near her, when asked by the Vicar if he had discovered the cause of the noises replied 'It's herself and the witches from Brailes, sir, as does it.' 'What, Thomas, do you, an educated man, believe such nonsense?' 'I know for a fact, sir, that she rides on her broomstick to Brailes every night. And she takes the form of a hare too – I have seen her myself running along by my garden fence.'

Another of the Brailes witches was called Nance. She had remarkable powers: if she disliked a girl she could suspend her from the ceiling by her hair, and if feeling really hateful could make her walk on it like a fly (this was told in 1914). Nance could turn herself into a white cat or rabbit and could place a spell on an oven door so that it would remain shut in spite of the most desperate attempts to get it open.

In 1880 a dairymaid from Willington who believed her cows to be under a spell took a sheep's heart, stuck it with pins, and roasted it in an oven. Thus the witch in one of her guises was drawn there. She was a tiny animal 'the like of which none of them had ever seen, that came and scratted at the stopless closing the oven door, trying to reach the heart'. The creature was killed and this ended the spell. A favourite place for fairy people or witches to appear was on the bacon rack to be found in every cottage chimney. The hams of the household pig were here preserved by the never-ending smoke of the fire, together with tubs of lard and other delicacies. Tiny witches were said to play around the edges of these racks, dancing merrily among the swirling smoke.

More obviously, the wych-elm was a home of the witch. She could be benevolent or malignant according to the behaviour of the people around her (*Warwickshire Press*, 6th October 1907). The inhabitants of the Forest of Arden knew of old women who lived in these beautiful old trees, now unhappily becoming extinct in this country. They also asserted that on very rare occasions the trunk of the tree splits open to reveal not an ugly old hag of a witch, but the most beautiful young girl imaginable who sings a melody of unearthly sweetness. For this reason the timber of the wych-elm was supposed to be sacred, and it was seldom used for manufacture or even firewood (a contributory factor may be that the wood is very difficult to split and does not burn well anyway). Anyone who failed to observe this practice would feel the evil power of the witch of the tree, and this could prove fatal.

Snowshill – A Lonely Village of the Hills

Snowshill

Snowshill – A Lonely Village of the Hills

Snowshill, as well as being one of the most beautiful villages of the Cotswolds, is also one of the most lonely. Its remote position must account for much of its charm, for being away from any main road it remains unspoilt, with its outskirts almost unblemished by modern housing. The village lies snug below the hillsides, its cottages tightly grouped around the church and the fifteenth-century Manor House. This beautiful house came up for sale during the First World War, and an advertisement for it was seen by Charles Wade, a wealthy young man then serving as a sapper in France. He was so taken by the photograph and description of the house that immediately on his return to England he visited Snowshill and was delighted to find the Manor as he had imagined it – a wonderful old house in semi-ruinous condition, tailor-made to suit his own extravagantly romantic nature.

Thus he bought the house and after being discharged from the army set about its restoration, purposefully ignoring such modern trappings as electricity, preferring to retain oil lamps and candles. He made his own living quarters in the outbuildings, the Manor itself being used solely to house his enormous collection of *objets d'art*, mechanical oddities, wonderful clocks, and many other more bizarre items. He was a human jackdaw, a strange man who enjoyed dressing up and startling visitors to the house by using its numerous secret doors and passageways to confront them unexpectedly. Nevertheless for all his eccentricities he was a generous benefactor to the village and none of its inhabitants like to hear anything said against him even though his beliefs embraced magic. In a room at the top of the house, inaccessible to the public, there is a pentagram on the floor and a wall decorated with other mystic symbols. When the National Trust took over the Manor this room contained a fantastic

Snowshill Manor

assortment of objects that might have belonged to an alchemist or wizard of the Middle Ages. These were later loaned to the Museum of Witchcraft formerly at Bourton-on-the-Water and now grace a similar collection at Boscastle in Cornwall. However, there seems to be no firm evidence that Charles Wade was ever an active participant in the Black Arts though one recent account hints that he was a vampire (*The Vampire's Bedside Companion* by Peter Underwood). Little is produced to support this, other than that Wade was an eccentric, with a sinister appearance that he liked to emphasise, who slept with 'an enormous preserved bat over his bed'. Anyone who has seen Wade's cramped and spartan sleeping accommodation at Snowshill will appreciate the absurdity of this. Certainly no one in the village had heard of lovely ladies climbing from vaults in the churchyard after sunset, or even of sheep found on the wolds with the neat incisions of a vampire's fangs in their throats.

Several people who come to Snowshill to visit the Manor have commented at the threshold that the house has a 'feeling' to it, and one or two have even refused to enter. When Charles Wade began restoring the rooms on the first floor he sent a small fragment of the timber to a celebrated lady clairvoyant at Brighton, without telling her where they came from. She wrote back:

Two houses upon a steep slope – the larger, lofty and
mysterious. In the lofty house in an upper room, late at
night there is a girl in a green dress of the seventeenth
century – she is greatly agitated – she paces anxiously up
and down the room – she doesn't live here and will not stay
the night.

Later Charles Wade discovered the story of the secret marriage that took place in an upper room of the house on St Valentine's Eve, 1604. Anne Parsons, a sixteen-year-old heiress, was forcibly married there to a fortune-seeker at the dead of night. She afterwards refused to stay in the house and the unhappy wedding party had to make a cold and dangerous night-time journey to Chipping Campden.

Another cause for psychic unrest here may be the result of a duel that once took place in the room called Zenith in which one

of the participants was killed. A further story tells how Charles Marshall lived in the house in the nineteenth century and held leases on over a thousand acres of land. After his death his widow continued to live at the Manor and farmed the land which went with the house. During this time Richard Carter, one of the labourers, was working at Hill Barn, a remote, high place linked to the village by a little-frequented track. On returning home one winter's evening he encountered the ghost of his former master, Charles Marshall, who rode alongside him mounted on a handsome black pony. After this had happened several times Carter told the rector who advised him to confront the ghost with the words 'What troublest thou here, in the Name of the Lord!'

When thus challenged the ghost said that Carter should meet him at midnight in the chaff-house. This he did and he was given a secret message for Mrs Marshall, the widow, the contents of which were never revealed. However, rumour had it that the message gave the location of hidden money since soon after the incident she was able to start new buildings to the north of the Manor. (This story was told to Charles Wade in 1919 by Richard Dark, son-in-law of Richard Carter).

Charles Wade gave Snowshill Manor to the National Trust in 1951 complete with his weird yet fascinating collection. He died five years later. It is his character that permeates the rooms that visitors see and the wonderful, fragrant garden that he created. He wrote of the house:

Old am I, so very old,
Here centuries have been.
Mysteries my walls enfold,
None know deeds I have seen.

Snowshill has other mysteries too. Mr Biles, once the landlord of the Snowshill Arms, often saw a strange figure in the ancient part of the inn upstairs. He denied that the apparition was ever the result of the unique properties of the Donnington ales that he sold, and said that it could open doors and would upset his dog, who would retreat to the more modern part of the building downstairs. The figure often resembled a hooded monk but sometimes had little shape at all, being just a miasmic form that would vanish through a wall or a closed door. It never showed animosity to Mr Biles or any of his family although the former never came to really believe in ghosts even though he saw this strange figure many times.

Finally there is the presence that lurks in the lane that runs past the Manor. There is a place here that many of the older inhabitants refuse to pass after nightfall. Local people believe that the ghost, like the one that haunts the pub, is that of an unhappy monk. In medieval times a Priory stood on the site of the Manor and the older part of the Snowshill Arms served as a hostel for visiting clergy and lay-people. The reason why these unfortunate churchmen should still haunt the locality is unknown.

Two Tales of Berkeley

Berkeley Castle

Two Tales of Berkeley

In later pages of this volume the reader will find parallels to the story of the Berkeley witch, and the manner of her being carried off by the Devil on an enormous black horse with (according to the account of William of Malmesbury) iron hooks projecting from its back. However, leaving aside Southey's ballad which was inspired by the story, the flavour of the legend is best captured by a local historian, John Smyth, who wrote the following in the early years of the seventeenth century, basing it on the translation of an even earlier source, the *Polychronicon* of Reinulph of Chester.

'About that time a certaine woman in Berkeley
accustomed to evil arts, when as upon a certaine day shee
kept a feast, a Chough which shee used delicately to feede
cackled more loudly and distinctly than shee was wont to
doe, which when shee heard, the knife fell out of her hand,
her countenance waxed pale, and having fetched a deepe
groane, with a sigh said, "now this day is the plowe come
to my last furrowe"; which beinge said, a messenger
coming in, declared to her the death of her sonne, and of
all her family exposed to present ruine; the woman
presently laye downe and called to such of her other
children as were monkes and a Nunne, who cominge shee
thus spake unto them: "I a wicked follower of an evil art
and worse life vainly thought to have been defended by
your praiers, now I desire to be eased by you of my
torments, because judgement is given against my soul, but
peradventure you may keepe my body if it bee fast sewed in
a stag's skin; make yee for mee a chest of stone, fast bound
and cemented with iron and lead, setting the same
upright, and also bound about with three iron chaines; use
singers of Psalms for forty nights and pay for soe many

masses by dayes; and if I shall soe lie for three nights, on
the fourth day bury my body in the ground." But all was in
vaine, for in the two first nights that the psalmes were in
soundinge, the Divells havinge easily broken the doores,
as lightly brake the two utmost iron chaines; and on the
third night about cock-crowinge, the place shakinge, one
with a terrible countenance and of a mighty tall stature,
havinge broken open the cover of the chest commanded the
dead body to arise, who answeringe that shee could not by
reason of the bonds; "bee thou loosed", quoth hee, "but to
thy woe"; and presently all the barres being broken, hee
draweth her out of the Church, and setteth her upon a
blacke horse, neighinge before the doore, and soe went
away with loud soundinge cries heard four miles off.'
Both versions of the story add a footnote which points out that
monks were commonly the authors of such legends, partly as a
warning to those tempted to undertake similar evil practices,
partly as a revenge against the dead. On occasions they would
even act out the drama around the coffin, dressed in appropriate
disguises. Such an episode is supposed to have occurred around
the corpse of Charles Martel, King of France.

To my mind there are few places in England with a more
sinister aura than Berkeley Castle. Most probably this feeling
derives from the hideous death suffered in its dungeons by
Edward II (he was slowly disembowelled in the most revolting
way possible: as he was homosexual the manner of his execution
probably appealed to the coarse sense of humour of his medieval
torturers). The Castle must have a hoard of spectacular ghosts,
but if it does I have failed to find them. However, the following
remarkable discovery, also from the account by John Smyth, goes
a little way to making up for this deficiency. The description of
the dungeon is very similar to the one shown to visitors as being
the scene of the murder of King Edward.

'Out of which dungeon in the likenes of a deepe broade
well goinge steepely down in the midst of the Dungeon
Chamber in the said Keepe, was (as tradition tells) drawne
forth a Toad, in the time of Kinge Henry the seventh, of an
incredible bignes, which, in the deepe dry dust in the

29

bottom thereof, had doubtlesse lived there divers hundreds of yeares; whose portraiture in just demension, as it was to me affirmed by divers aged persons, I sawe, about 48 years agone, drawne in colours upon the Doore of the Great Hall, and of the utter side of the stone porch leadinge into that hall; since, by pargettors or pointers of that wall washed out or outworne with time; which in bredth was more than a foot, neere sixteen inches, and in length more. Of which monstrous and outgrowne beast the inhabitants of this towne, and in the neighbour villages round about, fable many strange and incredible wonders; makinge the greatnes of this toad more than would fill a peck, yea, I have heard some, who looked to have beleife, say from the reports of their Fathers and Grandfathers that it would have filled a bushell or strike, and to have beene many yeares fed with flesh and garbage from the butchers; but this is all the trueth I knowe or dare believe.'

A Place for Ghosts and Witches?
Ilmington and District

The ruined church in Ettington Park

A Place for Ghosts and Witches?
Ilmington and District

Ilmington lies towards the northern edge of the Cotswolds, almost eight miles to the south of Stratford-upon-Avon. It is a village well-populated with ghosts, and, in days gone by, had its fair share of witches too. Its most spectacular ghost is probably the 'Night Coach' which is driven from Mickleton. The Coach always travels in this easterly direction and, driven by six horses, it is followed by a pack of spectral hounds.

There may be a connection between this and the next ghost which is of a man who lived in the village whose obsession was hunting. Because of this he even neglected his church-going. One night his hounds howled continuously so that in the end he was forced to go out of the house to quieten them. Unfortunately they failed to recognise him and he was torn to pieces. Ever since his ghost has gone a-hunting on Christmas Eve and on New Year's Day. 'If he sees anyone and gives a casual command, say, to open a gate, it must *not* be obeyed, or the person will fall into his power and be carried off for ever.' (G. Morley – *Shakespeare's Greenwood.*)

Another equestrian ghost haunts Pig Lane – it is a coach drawn by headless horses with a driver in the same condition, which carries the body of a ruthless local magnate who murdered a business rival. New Year's Eve is a busy time for the ghosts of Ilmington for the bells of the church have been known to ring out then to frighten away the Devil. The ghost of Edmund Golding, a parish clerk who died in 1793, haunts the church at midnight, wandering up and down restlessly muttering responses. It is many years since he has been seen.

There was a notorious place quite close to Ilmington on the Stratford road at the crossroads by Bruton Barn where farmers returning from Stratford market late at night would be held up. Their horses would refuse to budge and there they would sit,

sometimes for an hour or more. This was often blamed on Betty, the local witch, but may have had a more fearful reason as it was supposed to have been the burial-place for a highwayman who was particularly evil and was laid to rest here with a stake driven through his heart – the treatment more usually reserved for vampires or 'some unfortunate under the ban of the greater excommunication', whatever that means.

Betty lived at Darlingscot, the village just to the south of Ilmington, in the mid-nineteenth century. She used to cadge from her neighbours who at last grew tired of giving her free clothing and food and sent her packing. After this nothing would go right for them – the butter and cheese failed and even the fires refused to burn properly. She was said to take the shape of a hare at night and many attempts were made to shoot it; these were all unsuccessful though once it limped away wounded. The next day Betty was found laid up with a gammy leg. One night there was a tremendous thunderstorm and when the horses threatened to stampede in the yard the farmer and his groom went out to tie them up. They distinctly saw Betty ride off on a hurdle 'up and down, ridge and furrow' disappearing into the distance.

To the west of Ilmington is the village of Mickleton, sometimes troubled by a great booming noise made by a goblin known as the Mickleton Hooter. He occupies a small wood close to the village and frightens away poachers with his unearthly cries. Another theory is that the Hooter is the ghostly Dun Cow which once went berserk and was eventually killed by Guy of Warwick.

The church at Honington stands close to the main road between Stratford and Oxford. Another Old Betty haunts the churchyard here – sitting on the wall and smoking a pipe. When she was alive she often used to sit at the top of a withy (willow) tree disconcerting passers-by below by making a great display in pulling on her stockings. This eccentric old lady lived in a cottage midway between Honington and Tredington.

The church at the next village to the north, Halford, has a ghost that was seen by two young ladies in the winter of 1906–7. At the time an unconvincing explanation was given that the figure was that cast by the lectern. A spectral white calf has been seen on the road to Ettington which is also haunted by an old woman who wears a white sun-bonnet and carries a basket. A Roman burial-place was located close to this road and some gypsies committed a murder here long ago.

Ettington Park lies close to Halford on the main Stratford to Oxford road. The manor-house looks like the archetypal haunted house (it is now a hotel) with fairy-tale turrets and dark trees surrounding it. It was a seat of the Shirleys, one of the oldest of Warwickshire families, whose crest is to be seen above the enormous fireplace in the oldest, Tudor, part of the house. Close by are the entrances to two tunnels leading to secret rooms (priestholes). The severed head on the crest commemorates an incident when one of the Shirleys, provoked in an argument, struck off the head of his adversary and had it nailed to the front

Ettington Park

door of the house as a warning. The original door ran red with blood on the anniversary of this savagery. Appropriately, the house was used by Hammer Films for location work in *The Haunting*, one of their best efforts in the genre for which they are so famous.

A catalogue of the ghosts of Ettington Park might begin with the transparent lady in grey who may be seen in the Library or by the great stone staircase which leads from the hall. She usually appears at dusk and is said to be the ghost of a mistress of the house, pushed to her death at the foot of the stairs after an altercation with her maid. Other rooms in the house are also said to hold the restless spirits of the dead and an American tourist once took a photograph which showed a figure standing at one of the windows. The trouble was that the window in question was in a room that had no floor!

The ancient church that stands close to the house has a ghost that haunts its balcony. In the park two children are sometimes seen dressed in the clothes of a hundred years ago. They are the spirits of two members of the Shirley family tragically drowned while playing by the river.

The Worcestershire Wizard and the Witch of Evesham

Worcester Cathedral

The Worcestershire Wizard and the Witch of Evesham

We have already met with a variety of witches in an early chapter. Here are two more who appear to be typical characters of the seventeenth century. John Lambe was a rogue who used his knowledge of magic and the gullibility of the populace to build a reputation as a wise man, or wizard. He must have been a likeable rascal, however, for friends in high places allowed him to escape justice at the gallows twice, though it finally caught up with him when he was confronted by a street-mob and beaten to death. Catherine Huxley, the Witch of Evesham, is interesting for a different reason. She had no powerful friends to save her from the hangman, and her fate was shared by many hundreds of women unlucky enough to earn the dislike or mistrust of their neighbours.

At the Summer Assizes held at Worcester in 1652 Catherine Huxley, 'a single woman, aged about 40 years' was charged with bewitching Mary Ellins of Evesham, aged about nine years. In April of that year Mary had thrown stones at the woman and called her a witch. As she fled, Huxley shouted back that Mary herself would have stones enough, later. The girl almost immediately fell ill and about a month later 'began to void stones, which she continued to do until the witch was condemned and executed, when she made a rapid recovery'. This brief official account (quoted in *Witchcraft and Demonianism*) hardly does justice to the horror of the story, but it implies that the most telling piece of evidence against the witch only occurred after her execution. The case was included in a famous collection of stories of witches and ghosts written by Richard Baxter and first published in 1691. It was subsequently reprinted many times, even as recently as 1834 (when the Evesham account was omitted), being regarded as a classic text against the powers of witches. Its full title is *The Certainty of the Worlds of Spirits fully*

The death of the infamous Doctor Lambe

evinced by unquestionable Histories of Apparitions, Operations, Voices, etc., Proving the Immortality of Souls, the Malice and Miseries of the Devils and the Damned, and the Blessedness of the Justified. Written for the Conviction of Sadduces and Infidels.

Baxter was chaplain to the Commonwealth Armies during the early years of the Civil War, but later retired to Rous Lench under the patronage of Sir Thomas Rous. He became friendly with George Hopkins (the former vicar of Evesham, ejected for his nonconformity in 1662, who afterwards lived at Dumbleton to avoid the effects of the Five Mile Act). Hopkins related the story to Baxter, who described it as 'the certainest and fullest instance of witchcraft that ever I knew. . . .' This puts meat on the bones of the synopsis of the story related above.

The Narrative as lately sent me from most Credible Persons in Evesham is as followeth:

About the month of April, 1652, Mary, the Daughter of

Edward Ellins, of the Borough of Evesham, in the County of Worcester, gardner, then about nine or ten years old, went in the fields on a Saturday with some other children to gather cowslips, and finding in a Ditch by the wayside, at the said Town's end, one Catherine Huxley, a single woman, aged about forty years . . . the children called her Witch, and took up stones to throw at her, the said Mary also called her Witch, and took up a stone, but was so affrighted that she could not throw it at her; then they all run away from her, and the said Mary being hindmost, this Huxley said to her, 'Ellins you shall have enough stones in your stomach'. Whereupon Mary fell that day very ill and continued so weak and languishing that her Friends feared that she would not recover.

At this point the account differs from the previous one. As the child's health declined, the stones causing the trouble began to appear, until in the end there were eighty of them 'some plain pebbles, some plain flints, some very small, and some about an ounce weight'. After a month or so 'strong suspitions' began to be felt that Mary was bewitched and so Huxley was arrested, examined, and searched. At her bedhead stones similar to those already produced by Mary Ellins were found. This damning evidence brought poor Catherine Huxley to the gallows. After the execution Mary began to recover, ridding herself of even more stones. She subsequently had seven children and was still alive in 1691.

Her stones became famous and many people came to her family offering to buy them. In the end they grew tired of this and threw them away. Thomas Wriothesley, fourth Earl of Southampton and Lord High Treasurer of England, acquired a number of them. He had a morbid interest in the subject, suffering from the same complaint himself. In 1667 he decided against having a surgeon remove those with which he was afflicted but instead took the potion prepared by an old lady who dabbled in the dark arts. This draught was meant to dissolve the stones but instead proved 'very drastic' to the Earl, who died in agony but, mercifully, quite quickly.

There is also an irony in the fate of the father of George

40

Hopkins, the dissident clergyman who told the story of the Evesham Witch to Richard Baxter with such relish. The latter relates how Mr Hopkins told him 'as a great secret that he was possest (meaning, I think, Bewitcht); I chid him as Fanciful and Melancholy. He long continued in pain and in that conceit, and before he died he and his family had reason to think that a piece of wood the length of one's finger was the cause of his distemper.' Hopkins was sure that he had never swallowed such a thing, and his son adds as a footnote to his death how 'the best men it seems may be thus afflicted, as Job, by Satan'.

The Worcestershire Wizard was John Lambe who lived for a time at Tardebigg, near Bromsgrove. His early career was as a schoolteacher to the children of gentry, but he soon began to dabble in magic, becoming known for his skill at clairvoyance, telepathy, and medicine. He was also an accomplished juggler and entertainer, thus, it seems, possessing all the attributes to allow him to become established as the local wise man, who could help people out of all sorts of difficulties, at a price. However, not everybody appreciated these qualities and in 1609 he was called upon to answer several charges concerning his practices, two of them being:

On 16 Dec. 1607 at Tardebrigge, certain evil, diabolical, and execrable arts called witchcrafts, etc., in and upon the Rt. Hon. Thomas, Lord Windsor, devilishly did use, practixe and exercise, etc., to the intent to consume the body and strength of the said Thomas, Lord Windsor.

On 13 May 1608, at Henlipp (viz. Hindlip, just outside Worcester) did invoke and entertain evil spirits.

Fragments of the Crown's evidence on the second charge are quoted in *Witchcraft and Demonianism.*

The prosecution witness, Mr Wayneman, told how Lambe boasted that he would show him an angel, and attempted to conjure him up in a crystal glass placed on the crown of his hat set on a table. This was unsuccessful. He also claimed to Wayneman that he had powerful influences at his command that could poison or bewitch men so that they would be unable to beget children. He had four familar spirits 'bound to his crystal', the chief of which was named Benias. These he was able to use to hunt for mislaid valuables. Another gift he had was the ability to recognise a witch at a glance; he could also diagnose illness without even seeing the sufferer. Once, while giving a display of conjuring, he told Lady Fairfax that very soon water would bring her heartache. Three days later her brothers were drowned.

The self-styled doctor spent some time in Worcester Castle awaiting trial, but his imprisonment there seems not to have dampened his spirits at all. He had many visitors and surprised one for whom – asked by Lambe what he would like to drink and replying sack – he produced a pottle (half-gallon jug) immediately, which he claimed came from the Globe Tavern, half a mile away. The puzzled visitor later made enquiries at the Globe and found that at the time of the conversation a boy dressed in green had fetched wine for Doctor Lambe. On another occasion he and some friends were carousing when they saw a good-looking woman out walking. The 'Wizard' 'caused her to lift her coats above her middle' to the great amusement of his fellow revellers.

Lambe was eventually found guilty on both charges, but sentence was deferred since an outbreak of jail-fever affected many of those who took part in his trial. Altogether forty people died, including the High Sheriff and the foreman of the jury. Naturally Lambe's spells were thought to be the cause of this, and he was transferred to the King's Bench prison in London where he continued to live in style and comfort, entertaining many of the best-known people of the day, under the patronage of the Duke of Buckingham. In 1624 he was accused of the rape of a young girl, found guilty by jury, and sentenced to death. However, the influence of his powerful friends prevailed and he was set free. This brought his downfall, for in 1628, returning from a visit to the Fortune Theatre, he was set upon in the street by a mob and beaten to death.

'The Prodigious Noises of War'
– Edge Hill

Edge Hill Tower

'The Prodigious Noises of War' – Edge Hill

The Battle of Edge Hill took place near Kineton, just to the east of Stratford on Sunday, 23 October 1642. It was the first major engagement of the Civil War and ended with both sides claiming victory. The Royalists had had the better of the fight at first after a great cavalry charge led by Prince Rupert. He went on to pursue the Roundheads' baggage-train, leaving his foot-soldiers to fend for themselves on the battlefield. At this point the Parliamentary forces rallied and began to cut through the abandoned Royalist infantry who were only saved from annihilation by the last-minute return of the Prince. At the end of the day honours were even and a thousand lay dead on the field.

On the Christmas Eve following this awful event 'shepherds and other countrymen, together with certain wayfarers' were amazed to find themselves in the thick of a ghostly re-enactment of the battle. Between midnight and one in the morning they heard 'first the sound of drums afar off and the noises of soldiers, as it were, giving out their last groans'. This dreadful disturbance grew louder and louder, closer and closer, until the battle seemed to rage all about them – guns firing, horses neighing in distress, and men screaming and shouting. Then the whole scene suddenly became visible and the two sides were clearly identified by the colours being carried and worn. The battle went on for a considerable time, until at last one side was seen to fall back leaving the field to their foes who seemed to be rejoicing in victory. The frightened witnesses to the event persuaded more villagers to accompany them to the scene the following, Christmas, night, when the battle took place in exactly the same manner as it had the night before.

Word was next sent to the local Justice of the Peace and to the Minister, who was his neighbour. At first these worthies were incredulous but the vehemence with which the story was told led

them to keep vigil during the nights following. The ghostly armies reappeared a week after the first re-enactment of the battle. The Justice and many others who were present 'forsook the place utterly, believing it accursed' but the Minister sat through the whole terrible spectacle, his faith in the Lord unshaken.

These strange events soon became known throughout the troubled kingdom. The King himself, then at Oxford, sent high-ranking officers to investigate. They stayed at Kineton for a week 'wherein they heard and saw the forementioned prodigies, distinctly knowing divers of the apparitions, or incorporeal substances, by their faces, as that of Sir Edmund Varney and others that were slain, of which upon oath they made testimony to his Majesty'. (This, like the earlier quotes, is from a contemporary pamphlet.)

The amazing confirmation of a story first put about by 'shepherds and countrypeople' gives the ghostly battle an authenticity important to the student of similar events. These have been reported from other locations in Britain, notably at Culloden (the scene of the massacre of the followers of Prince Charles Edward Stuart) where an 'army in the sky' has appeared. There may be a parallel here with the Herlethingi (the companies of the undead) of the Continent. The following is from Anthony Masters' *Natural History of the Vampire*; he quotes an ancient account by Walter Map:

In Brittany there used to be seen at night long trains of
soldiers who passed by in dead silence conducting
carriages of booty, and from these the Breton peasants
have actually stolen away horses and cattle and kept them
for their own use. In some cases no harm seems to have
resulted, but in other instances this was speedily followed
by sudden death. Companies of these troops of night-
wanderers, who are commonly called *Herlethingi*, were
very well known in England even to the present day, the
reign of our King Henry II, who is now ruling over us.
These armies went to and fro without let or stay, hurrying
hither and thither rambling about in the most mad
vagrancy, all inceding in unbroken silence, and amongst

the band there appeared alive many who were known to have been long since dead. This company of *Herlethingi* last espied in the Marches of Hereford and Wales in the first year of King Henry II, tramping along at high noon with carts and beasts of burden, with pack saddles and provender-baskets, with birds and dogs and a mixed multitude of men and women. Those who first caught sight of this troop by their shouting and blowing of horns and trumpets aroused the whole district, and as in the manner

47

of those border folk, who are ever on the watch, almost instantly there assembled various bands fully equipped, and because they were unable to obtain a word in reply from this strange host they incontinently prepared to make them answer to a shower of darts and javelins, and then the troop seemed to mingle with the air and forthwith vanish away out of sight. From that day this mysterious company has never been seen by man.

Only occasionally are there reports of anything untoward happening on Edge Hill today. There are claims that the re-enactment of the battle still occurs each year on 23 October, but more commonly the ghost of Prince Rupert is seen on his white charger accompanied by a small dog. He revisits the place where his blunder in pursuing the riches contained in the opposing baggage-train robbed him of a decisive victory. Any supernatural battle occurring today might well be confused with a mock one staged by the Sealed Knot.

The Murder of Charles Walton

Charles Walton

The Murder of Charles Walton

From the *Stratford-upon-Avon Herald* of 16 February 1945:

Warwickshire police are investigating what may prove to be a murder of a particularly brutal character.

On Wednesday night, following a search, the body of a 74-year-old farm labourer, Mr Charles Walton, of Lower Quinton, was found with terrible injuries in a field on Meon Hill, where he had been engaged in hedge-laying.

A trouncing-hook and a two-tined pitch fork are said to have been embedded in his body.

Mr Walton, who lived with his niece, was a frail old man. He suffered considerably from rheumatism and walked with the aid of two sticks.

LONELY SPOT

However, he still did odd jobs for local farmers, and on Wednesday morning set off to work at the Hill grounds, a lonely spot about a mile from his home. When his niece, Miss Walton, returned from work at about 6 p.m., she found that the old man had not been in for dinner, for which he normally returned at about 4 p.m. She notified a neighbour, Mrs Beasley, fearing that he had fallen. Accompanied by Mr Potter, of The Firs (for whom Mr Walton was working), and Mr Beasley, she set off for the field where Walton had been employed. Mr Potter made the tragic discovery.

NO ENEMIES

Mr Walton spent his whole life in Quinton, and was known to everyone. The tragedy has shocked the locality.

A neighbour told the *Herald* that he was a quiet, inoffensive old man, 'one of the best you would meet in a day's march,' and he was not likely to have had any enemies in the village.

'He always had a cheery word for everyone,' she said.

It seems impossible to impute any motive for murder.

Mr Potter, who found the body

Miss Walton is engaged to a Stratford man, and following the discovery of the tragedy left her home for Stratford.

Last night the police were continuing their inquiries and had visited a camp in the area.

Later it was stated that the police regard the crime as the work of a lunatic or someone maddened by drink.

On the following Friday the *Herald* reported the inquest:

Inquiries are being continued by Chief Inspector Fabian and Det.-Sergt. Webb, of Scotland Yard, who arrived in Stratford-on-Avon on Friday to investigate the brutal murder of Mr Charles Walton, of Lower Quinton, the 74-year-old farm worker whose terribly mutilated body was found in a ditch on Meon Hill, where he had been working.

The billhook and hayfork that were found embedded in the body had been used ferociously. Three definite slashes were made with the hook, while the fork had been driven through the neck, pinning the body to the ground. A blood-stained walking stick was found near, and bruises on the head suggested the old man was struck first with it. That he had made efforts to defend himself was apparent from cuts on his hand.

Charles Walton lived in this cottage

.TD.

Stratford-upon-Avon H[

AND SOUTH WARWICKSHIRE ADVERTISER

I wish no other *Herald*,
No other speaker of my living actions.—*Shakespeare*.   FRIDAY, FEBRUARY 16, 1945   Registered at the General

CHEME: COUNTY RVE JUDGMENT

OMPARE WITH THAT LOPTON BRIDGE?

"I have been in this thing for the last 20 years," said Alderman T. H. RYLAND, amid laughter.

He recalled that 21 years ago a County Council agreed on a scheme for widening Clopton Bridge and it was decided that it could be done. Then, unfortunately, societies came along and intervened, causing differences between the County Council and Stratford-on-Avon. All the way through there had been two issues—whether to widen the existing bridge or to have a new one—but the main question had been one of finance. He thought it only reasonable that before they sanctioned any

OLD MAN'S TERRIBLE INJURIES

Inflicted with Billhook and Pitchfork

TRAGIC DISCOVERY AT QUINTON

Warwickshire police are investigating what may prove to be a murder of a particularly brutal character.

On Wednesday night, following a search, the body of a 74-year-old farm labourer, Mr. Charles Walton, of Lower Quinton, was found with terrible injuries in a field on Meon Hill, where he had been engaged in hedge-laying.

A trouncing hook and a two-tined pitch fork are said to have been embedded in his body.

Mr. Walton, who lived with his niece, was a frail old man. He suffered

TWO LOADS FOR SHOREDITCH

Miss Melville (local W.V.S. organiser) states that two loads (eight tons) of household goods have been sent from Stratford-on-Avon and district to Shoreditch, and she hopes that another will be despatched next Tuesday. So far the only other place to send two loads is Sutton Coldfield. Gifts are still being received. A crate of china, worth £74, has also been bought and sent direct from the Pottery district, and this will be added to Stratford and district total.

Miss Melville has received a letter from Miss Gammon (the W.V.S. organiser for Shoreditch) in which she says: "Your two loads have arrived and are just marvellous. I think it is amazing of people to send us all this lovely stuff,. which they must need themselves, but I cannot tell you how we appreciate it here and what a joy

SU

Professor J. M. Webster (West Midland Forensic Laboratory) read an extensive report dealing with the condition of the various organs and the injuries, and gave the cause of death as shock and haemorrhage, due to grave injuries to the neck and chest caused by a cutting weapon and a stabbing weapon.

He added that the cutting weapon was wielded three times and that the old man had attempted to defend himself. Ribs were broken and the front of the old man's clothing was undone. All the great blood vessels of the neck were severed. Walton was a remarkably healthy man for his age.

The inquest was adjourned.

This brief account from the local paper sketches an outline of the brutal murder that took place at Lower Quinton thirty-five years ago and remains unsolved today. It still brings investigators to the quiet village and one of the policemen originally involved in the case, Det.-Supt. Spooner, revisited the scene every year on the anniversary of the crime until his retirement fifteen years later. Most probably he thought that the publicity would eventually awaken the local conscience and at last someone would come forward with information which would lead to the conviction of the killer of Walton, who seemed at first a harmless old recluse.

As investigations continued, however, hints of more sinister motives for the killing were uncovered. Reference has already been made to the chapter on witchcraft in J. Harvey Bloom's *Folklore of Shakespeare's Land*. One of the incidents mentioned there provides the first of the coincidences which abound in this case: 'At Alveston a plough lad named Charles Walton met a dog[1] on his way home nine times in successive evenings. He told both the shepherd and the carter with whom he worked and was laughed at for his pains. On the ninth encounter a headless lady rustled past him in a silk dress, and on the next day he heard of his sister's death.' Now Alveston is on the opposite side of Stratford from Lower Quinton, about six miles distant as the crow flies, and it was not until 1968 that a connection was made between the two stories. In his book on the Walton murder Donald McCormick states that the haunting took place in 1885, when Walton would have been about fourteen, and an Alveston man confirmed that the same Charles Walton was involved. After this, he said, Walton, who had been 'a real chatterbox', became a man of few words, taciturn to those he knew and surly with strangers.

The murder was committed on St Valentine's Day, 14 February. By another of those strange coincidences that plague the case this was also the first day of February by the old calendar – the day when the Druids performed human sacrifice in order to ensure the fertility of their fields. It was also Ash Wednesday.[2]

[1] Dogs, especially black ones which portend ill-fortune and death, seemed to play a role in the story. Soon after the murder a black dog was found hanging from a tree near the murder spot. The Chief Inspector investigating Walton's death ('Fabian of the Yard') had a strange encounter with a large black dog which he mentioned in the village pub. Subsequently a police car was involved in an accident with another black dog.

[2] Dr Margaret Murray, the famous Professor of Egyptology of London University, who was fascinated by this murder, worked out the date to be 2 February by the old calendar. This, she said, was equally portentous. She visited Lower Quinton in 1950 to make her own investigations and told a *Birmingham Post* reporter that the pitchfork had been used after his death to force back the head so that blood could more easily reach the soil from his slashed throat. Professor Murray was eighty at the time of the murder and lived to be over a hundred.

54

Although few people in the village could claim friendship with the old man, many held him in respect for his understanding of animals and his knowledge of nature. He would feed wild birds from his hands and could intimidate angry dogs with a glance. After his death quirks like these were remembered and, perhaps, embroidered. Stories were told of him harnessing toads to draw a toy plough across the fields. The only item missing from his body was his watch-case. The chain that held it hung from his waistcoat, but the watch-case itself only came to light in August 1960 when outbuildings were demolished behind Walton's cottage. The police had made a thorough search for it after the murder, both in the fields and hedgerows and at his home so its loss seemed yet another coincidence. He kept a strange piece of dark glass inside the case about which he was very secretive. Local people subsequently thought it might be a 'witches' mirror' though its purpose was unexplained.

After a while the investigators came across another parallel. This was the way in which the murderer had followed the pattern of James Heywood's killing of Ann Turner in 1875 (see page 16). She too was pinned to the ground with a pitchfork before her throat was slashed with two strokes making a cross. She was killed by Heywood (more or less the village idiot) in the belief that she brought ill to the place (and death to some of its inhabitants) by the use of her evil eye.

Many of the villagers certainly thought that Walton was a 'rum 'un' even before his death. Possibly he made use of a person's credulity for his own amusement, running toads across their land so that they believed that he was blighting their crops and bringing them to ruin. Certainly this was a well-known spell: first mention of it is to be found in the account of the trial of Isabell Gowdie, the celebrated Scottish witch, in 1622. She confessed that her coven often used this curse:

Before Candlemas we went by East Kinloss, and then we yoked a plewghe of paddokis (*frogs or toads*). The divill held the plewghe, and John Younge in Mebestone, our officer, did drwe the plewghe. Paddokis did draw the plewghe as oxen, quickens (*twitch-grass*) were somes (*traces*), a ram's horn was a cowter; and a piece of ram's

55

horn was a sok (*yoke*). We went two several times about; and all we of the covin went still up and downe with the plewghe praying to the divill for the fruit of that land, and that thistles and briers might grow there.

Thus a slightly simple farmer, raised in a countryside where belief in witchcraft was far from dead, might have been seriously disturbed by old Charles' malignant looks (perhaps accompanied by the use of the witches' mirror). Then if misfortunes followed who could be the scapegoat but the old man himself? To appease the old gods his blood had better run into the soil to exorcise the evil. If the majority of the villagers who knew of the teasing ways of the old man and sympathised with his victim kept silent, then who would ever know who killed him? It was the total silence of the locals that baffled Chief Inspector Fabian and led to this being one of the few cases on his file to remain open. Most of the villagers who may have known the true identity of the killer are now dead so that the murder of Charles Walton is likely to stay an unsolved mystery.

The Cheltenham Ghost

St Annes, Pittville Circus Road

The Cheltenham Ghost

Until the late B. Adby Collins' book on the subject appeared in 1950 this was known as 'The Morton Ghost' as before then both the location of its appearance and the names of the people involved were deliberately kept secret. In fact the property is a large Victorian house standing in Pittville Circus Road called St Anne's. It is now divided into flats and there have been no reports of anything untoward happening at the address since 1962.

When the house was put up in 1860 it was advertised by its speculative builder as 'a typical modern residence, square and common place in appearance'. It was bought by a Mr Swinhoe who lived there happily until the death of his wife, to whom he was devoted. After two years as a widower, during which time he drank heavily, he re-married. His new wife, Imogen, thought that the happiness that she would bring him would take away his need for the bottle. Unhappily she was wrong in this and in fact his drinking became worse. This so depressed her that she too began to drink and in time became almost an alcoholic. There were frequent violent quarrels, many of them concerning Mr Swinhoe's first wife's jewellery which, it was later disclosed, he had hidden under the floorboards of the front room as a nest-egg for the children of his first marriage. Imogen left her husband before his death in July 1876 and went to live at Clifton. She never returned to the house, dying at Clifton on 23 September 1878. Curiously, in view of the unhappiness of her life there, she left instructions for her body to be buried at Cheltenham and her remains are in a churchyard situated within a quarter of a mile of the house. The cause of her death was given as 'Dipsomania – six months; sub-acute gastritis – one week'.[1]

[1] Sir Charles Oman, one of the most distinguished historians of the day, knew the family and, as President of the Oxford Psychical Society, took a keen interest in the case. Shortly before his death in 1946 he wrote to Adby Collins:

After Swinhoe's death the house was bought by an elderly gentleman who lived there for only six months before dying suddenly. His widow moved out and the house stood empty for four years in spite of being offered at a rent half of that usually asked for such a property.

In 1882 the house was at last let to a Captain Despard. He changed its name to 'Garden Reach' and in April of that year began a tenancy that was to last for ten years, despite the regular attentions of the resident ghost who first appeared soon after the family moved into the house, in June 1882. It was most often seen by the eldest daughter, Rosina, who kept a most meticulous account of the haunting which she sent in the form of a journal to a friend in the north of England, Catherine Campbell. This journal was used in the initial investigation of the case, undertaken by Frederick Myers – one of the founders of the Society for Psychical Research and later its Honorary Secretary. He was given access to all of the material sent by Rosina to Catherine which, unhappily, was subsequently lost. This allowed him to write up the case in detail in Volume VIII of the Proceedings of the Society with the name of the family changed to Morton and the location of the house concealed.

The ghost was only seen by five of the ten people who lived in the house during the years of the haunting, though it was also occasionally seen by servants and visitors. In addition twenty further people heard it (many of those who hear a ghost are too frightened to investigate further). Remarkably neither Captain Despard nor his invalid wife ever saw the ghost. One theory popular with later investigators was that the ghost was really Despard's mistress whom he was attempting to conceal from his family and servants. Possibly Rosina's description of her first encounter with the ghost supports this theory:

'Yes, I know all about the Despard haunting but not so much from their point of view as from that of the ghost.

'My mother was a resident in Cheltenham and I frequently stayed with her. She was a friend of Mrs Swinhoe and knew all about the tribulations from her dipsomaniac husband who was a retired Army Surgeon if I remember aright. The wonder was that she endured his violent fits so long – she had a bout of absolute danger from him. After his death she had something like a breakdown and finally left Cheltenham. She did not survive very long and did not die in the house where she had been so unhappy.'

'I had gone up to my room, but was not yet in bed, when I
heard someone at the door, and went to it, thinking it
might be my mother. On opening the door, I saw no one;
but on going a few steps along the passage, I saw the figure
of a tall lady, dressed in black, standing at the head of the
stairs. After a few moments she descended the stairs, and I
followed for a short distance, feeling curious what it could
be. I had only a small piece of candle, and it suddenly
burnt itself out; and being unable to see more, I went back
to my room.'

Surely this matter-of-fact reaction to the discovery of a strange
person roaming about the house at the dead of night is
unconvincing? Even if Rosina realised immediately that the
figure was that of a ghost it is remarkable that she just returned
quietly to her room to continue her interrupted sleep. Few girls of
her age (Rosina was twenty) would have failed to raise the hue
and cry in either case. Her account continues with a detailed
description of the figure:

'. . . a tall lady, dressed in black of a soft woollen material,
judging from the slight sound in moving. The face was
hidden by a handkerchief held in the right hand. This is all
I noticed then; but on further occasions when I was able to
observe her more closely, I saw the upper part of the left
side of the forehead, and a little of the hair above. Her left
hand was nearly hidden by her sleeve and a fold of her
dress. As she held it down, a portion of the widow's cuff
was visible on both wrists, so that the whole impression
was that of a lady in widow's weeds. There was no cap on
the head, but the general effect of blackness suggests a
bonnet, with long veil, or a hood.'

Other later descriptions of the ghost remain remarkably faithful
to this. Its route through the house was also consistent though it
reacted in different ways to material things or to people. It sat at a
writing-table, bent over one of Rosina's sisters when she was at
the piano as though about to turn over the page of the music that
she was playing and when spoken to she would give a slight gasp
as though she was attempting an answer, but would then turn
away. Perhaps the most distinctive characteristic of the

Cheltenham Ghost was its willingness to appear at any time of day or night, indoors or out. Significantly perhaps, in view of the Captain Despard's mistress theory, is the feeling of solidity that all witnesses claimed to have felt about the figure. This was a ghost that could be mistaken for a real human being, not a thing of mist and shadow, though some claimed that the air turned chill about them when the ghost was about. Its footsteps were very recognisable but on several occasions a second set of steps were heard 'heavy and irregular' which were accompanied by bumps and thuds. Bedroom doors frequently opened by themselves and the handles were often rattled. When Rosina and her brothers and sisters waited intentionally to see the ghost it would not appear. It easily avoided stratagems to trap it, such as threads across the stairs: it simply glided through them. Rosina wrote:

'I also attempted to touch her but she always eluded me. It was not that there was nothing to touch but that she always seemed to be *beyond* me, and if followed into a corner, simply disappeared.'

The garden front

Once children made a ring around the ghost, but it just walked out between two people and vanished. Dogs were sensitive to its presence, cats failed to react at all.

At the beginning of the haunting the ghost had a very substantial shape. As the visitation went on it became less distinct. After 1886 people could never mistake it for a real person, and although the ghost was not seen after 1889 light footsteps were heard until 1892.

In an appendix to his book Adby Collins tells of uncovering a revival of the haunting which occurred in 1903. He found a lady who had seen the ghost several times in the front garden. Later the house was used as a private school but the proprietors were at length forced to abandon it because of 'constant trouble from the ghost'.

St Anne's was eventually turned into flats, one of which was occupied by a Mr Thorne between 1957 and 1962. He frequently saw and heard a ghost in the building and relatives of his, who borrowed the flat in 1962, were driven out by a particularly violent experience. Since then there have been no further reports of trouble and the house appears smart and serene, giving the observer few hints of the dramas that its walls have witnessed.

The Rollright Stones

The King's Men, the Rollright Stones

The Rollright Stones

A local saying of a hundred years ago told how there were enough witches in Long Compton to draw a wagon-load of hay up Long Compton Hill. There are few wagon-loads of hay climbing the hill today – instead great articulated lorries grind up it, their noise shattering the peace of a lovely village. Close by, on a hilltop away from the main road to the south of the village, are the Rollright Stones – a great meeting-place of witches in the old days. A little way from the stone circle which, known as the King's Men, is the main feature of the site, there is a single upright stone – the Kingstone. A third group of stones is even further away to the east – these are called the Whispering Knights.

A famous legend tells how they acquired these names. Long, long ago a powerful king invaded England and eventually reached the far side of the hill which overlooks Long Compton. As he and his army climbed the hill a witch[1] appeared who happened to own this land. She stopped them all by chanting the words:

'Seven long strides shalt thou take, and
If Long Compton thou canst see,
King of England thou shalt be.'

And so the King confidently strode forward the seven paces but as he did so a great mound of earth rose up, blocking his view of the village, and the Witch concluded her chant:

'As Long Compton thou canst not see
King of England thou shalt not be.

[1] One source states that the witch was known as Mother Shipton as she came from the village of Shipton-under-Wychwood. It stresses that she had nothing to do with her more famous Yorkshire namesake even though, like her, she predicted that the world would end in 1881. This was believed by many country people throughout England and many a villager in the Cotswolds remembered the prophecy when they looked out on the unrelenting snowstorm that hit the area that winter.

Rise up stick, and stand still stone,
For King of England thou shalt be none,
Thou and thy men hoar stones shall be
And I myself an elden tree.'

Whereupon the King and his army were all turned into stones, the King below the crest of the mound and his men behind him. Close by was an elder tree. The Whispering Knights were traitors plotting the downfall of the King standing furtively out of earshot. They too were petrified.

The stones have magical properties. Fairies dance around the Kingstone on nights when there is a full moon. The Knights tell of the future if you have ears sensitive enough to hear their whispers. Some day the spell will be broken and all of the stones will become flesh again. The King will vanquish all his enemies and eventually rule over all the world.

More prosaically guidebooks tell us that the Rollright Stones are a Stone Circle of the Bronze Age dating from before 1500 BC. The main circle – the King's Men – was used 'for funerary ceremonial purposes but certainly had nothing to do with the later Druids'. However, witches still found the place exceptionally suitable for summoning up their masters of the evil craft and it was a regular venue for their sabbaths. It is still a sinister place, even in broad daylight. J. Harvey Bloom's classic, *Folk Lore, Old Customs and Superstitions in Shakespeare's Land*, published in 1929, mentions two incidents which show the magical power of the place. In the first a young farmer tells of the impossibility of keeping any gate shut around the Stones. Gates left closed in the evening, some even fastened by padlocks, would be found wide open in the morning. This gave a livestock farmer real problems. Another farmer told how his father once wished to bridge over a culvert near his house and to do so tried to move one of the stones down the hill using a strong team of heavy horses. These acted as though they were terrified, breaking out into a 'malt sweat' and failing to move the stone more than a few yards. Later a single horse was able to draw the stone back up the hill to its old position. The Stones are supposed to go down to the stream to drink on New Year's Eve (perhaps accounting for why the gates are left open, at least on one day of the year!). Students of

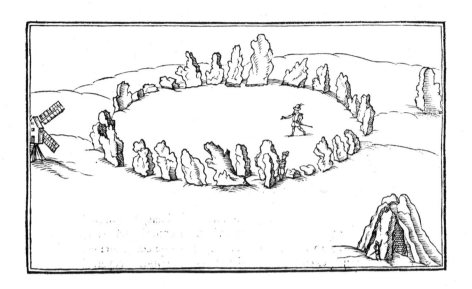

ley lines, earth energy and so on find this an important site (the ley leads through Wroxton and Copredy to Arbury Camp). A dowser has found 'overground energy' lines connecting the stones and continuing on into the countryside (see *The Ley Hunter's Companion* by Devereux and Thomson).

The Campden Wonder

Chipping Campden

The Campden Wonder

Chipping Campden is one of the most perfect of Cotswold villages and for this reason it attracts many thousands of visitors each year who gaze at the lovely old buildings and conjure up romantic thoughts of the happiness of the people who lived here three, four, or even five centuries ago. Yet however perfect the surroundings, the lives of ordinary people are rarely untroubled, and in times of political unrest even the most humble villager could find the habits of a lifetime upset and the neighbourhood in turmoil.

So it was after the collapse of the Cromwellian regime in 1659. The Puritan rise to power had left an indelible mark on the village. Rather than allow his magnificent home to fall into their hands, the third Viscount Campden had set fire to Campden House, and apart from one wing it was left a sad ruin. At the time of the events related here this wing was occupied by his mother, Juliana, the dowager Lady Campden. Her husband had died many years previously, her son was abroad, and she relied on her steward, William Harrison, for the day-to-day running of her estates which extended beyond Campden to the outlying hamlets.

It was one of the responsibilities of William Harrison to collect rents from these farms and on the afternoon of Thursday, 16 August 1660, he left Campden for Charringworth, about two miles away. It was sensible to leave late in the day as the farms and cottages would be deserted until evening when the men had finished harvesting. Harrison was a man respected by the community, aged about seventy. When he had failed to return by dusk his wife sent off their servant, John Perry, to look for him. He too failed to return and at dawn the next morning Harrison's son, Edward, also joined the search. He met Perry coming from Charringworth, and together they called at Ebrington, a village between the two places. The tenants there had certainly seen Mr Harrison the previous evening, for he had called there on the way back from Charringworth. They returned to Campden, and on the way heard a rumour that a collar and comb had been found by a poor woman out gleaning. These were identified as belonging to the steward and she took the search-party to the place where she had found them, opposite a great bank of furze which almost blocked the path at one point. By this time most people were certain that Harrison had met with some terrible accident as there were bloodstains on the collar and the comb was hacked and dented. Most people assumed that he had been murdered for the money he was carrying.

The search was unsuccessful. Mrs Harrison was suspicious of John Perry. Why hadn't he returned during the night? The next day he was called before the magistrates. He said that the darkness of the night made it impossible for him to reach Charringworth; he had first slept in a hen-roost. When the moon rose after midnight he had again set out but it turned suddenly

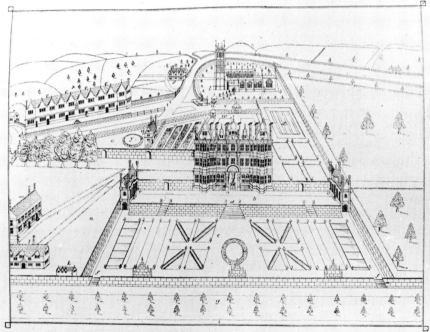

BIRDSEYE VIEW OF CAMPDEN HOUSE, BURNT DOWN IN THE YEAR OF NASEBY, 1645 (from an old drawing).

References—*a* The house. *b* The terrass walk. *c* The banquiting house. *d* The garden staires. *e* The great garden. *f* The orchart staires. *g* The great orchart. *i* The long canal. *k* The coach-house. *l* The brew-house. *m* The stables. *n* The stable court. *o* The henn yard. *p* The hospital. *q* The laundry. *r* The bleach garden. *s* The parsonage house. *t* The church. *u* The porter's lodge. *v* The outward court. *w* The great court. *x* The garden court. *y* The pond.

foggy and he sheltered in a ditch for the rest of the night. Two villagers confirmed that they had seen him near Campden soon after dusk. At daybreak he had continued his journey and woke up Edward Plaisterer, a tenant who occupied one of the cottages on the Campden side of the village. Plaisterer told Perry that he had given his master £23 the previous afternoon. Another resident of Charringworth, William Curtis, confirmed that Harrison had been there. On this, said Perry, he turned back to Campden and met Harrison's son on the way.

The Justice of the Peace asked why he had not returned to Mrs Harrison at midnight to see whether his master had arrived back. Perry explained unconvincingly that from the hen-roost he could see Harrison's chamber and since a light shone there he knew that he had not returned. Perhaps it was this that convinced the magistrate that Perry should be held in custody and so he was remanded for a week, lodged in an inn for part of the time and in the common jail for the remainder. He behaved strangely, telling some that a tinker had killed Harrison, others that a gentleman's servant had robbed him, then committed murder, and afterwards hidden the body in a bean rick. This latter was pulled apart but no sign of the corpse was found. He was again brought before the justice and remanded for a further week. At the end of this period he promised to tell the truth if he could see the magistrate a third time, and this time the story that he told caused a sensation.

Perry alleged that his mother and brother had killed Harrison. He had told them of the steward's likely movements that evening and they waylaid him at a lonely place called the Conygree where he was robbed and murdered. He arrived to find them with the steward on the ground. 'Ah, rogues, will you kill me?' he had cried. Despite pleas for his life from John Perry, his brother had brutally strangled him. Together they carried the body to the great Sink (cesspit) of Campden House. His brother and mother then told him to go to make sure no one was coming and he went as far as the Court Gate where he met and talked with John Pearce who had testified to this at the earlier hearing.

Perry admitted that he 'planted' the collar, hat and comb in the lane between Campden and Charringworth, having first scored

70

and stained them. Joan and Richard Perry, his mother and brother, were immediately arrested and the Sink dragged for the missing corpse. When this was unsuccessful the fish-ponds were also searched as were the ruins of Campden House. Both of the newly arrested Perrys denied the charges vigorously, accusing their kinsman of lying, yet he persisted in his allegations and so all three were remanded for trial at the Assize. On their way back to Campden from the house of the Justice 'a remarkable Circumstance' occurred which was to have dire consequences for all of the accused. Richard Perry was at the rear of the party when he pulled a handkerchief from his pocket. The 1676 account of the 'Wonder' describes how at the same time a ball of inkle (linen tape) fell to the ground 'which, one of his Guard taking up, he desired him to restore, saying, It was only his Wife's Hair-lace; but the Party opening of it, and finding a Slip-knot at the end, went and shewed it unto John, who was then a good distance before, and knew nothing of the dropping and taking up of the Inkle; but being shewed it, and asked, whether he knew it, shook his head and said, Yea, to his sorrow, for that was the String his Brother strangled his Master with. This was sworn upon the Evidence at their Trial.'

A second strange happening occurred on the following day: 'The Morrow being the Lord's-day, they remained at Campden, where the Minister of the Place designing to speak to them (if possible to persuade them to Repentance, and a further Confession) they were brought to Church; and in this way thither, passing by Richard's House, two of his children meeting him, he took the lesser in his arm, leading the other in his Hand; when, on a sudden, both their noses fell a bleeding, which was looked upon as ominous.'

Next in the account summarised here, possibly related by the very magistrate who examined the accused, Sir Thomas Overbury, who at this time lived close to Campden at Weston Subedge, there are two interesting 'Digressions'. The first tells how, the year previously, Mr Harrison's house had been 'broken open', the thieves gaining access by means of a ladder to an upstairs window. They took 'Seven Score Pounds in Money' (£140) which was never recovered. Not many weeks before the

71

disappearance of Mr Harrison his servant John Perry was found in the garden of Campden House, making a great outcry, with a pitchfork in his hand. He said that two men in white had set upon him with naked swords. The handle of the pitchfork confirmed this story, being deeply hacked and scored. When questioned about these incidents, John Perry said that the money had been stolen by his brother; he had been at Church at the time but had told him where the money was hidden and where the ladder was kept. It was to be hidden in the garden and shared out at Michaelmas. However, no trace of the cash was found. On being examined on the second episode Perry admitted it was 'a Fiction' which he had made up so that people would think that it was the mysterious 'men in white' who robbed his master and not himself.

The first trial took place in September. The Perrys faced two charges: that they robbed Harrison of £140, and, secondly, that they robbed and killed him subsequently. The judge dismissed this second charge saying that since a body had never been found murder could not be proved. At first all three pleaded Not Guilty to the remaining charge, but, prompted by lawyers who wanted to get the case dealt with quickly, they later changed their pleas to Guilty claiming that the Act of Oblivion pardoned them. This was Charles II's Bill of Indemnity and Oblivion which annulled all offences committed during 'the recent troubles'. For some unexplained reason this failed to bring about their acquittal and they remained in custody until the Spring Assizes of the following year. During this time John Perry continued to tell of the guilt of his mother and brother and even accused them of trying to poison him in jail.

However, all three pleaded their innocence at the second trial where they were brought before Sir Robert Hyde. The jury were unconvinced and found them guilty and Sir Robert duly sentenced all three to be hung. Sir Thomas Overbury describes the execution:

Some few days after, being brought to the Place of their
Execution, which was on Broadway-hill, in sight of
Campden; the Mother (being reputed a Witch, and to have
so bewitched her Sons, they could confess nothing, while

72

she lived) was first executed; after which, Richard, being upon the Ladder, professed, as he had done all along, that he was wholly innocent of the Fact for which he was then to die, and that he knew nothing of Mr Harrison's Death, nor what was become of him; and did, with great Earnestness beg and beseech, his Brother, for the Satisfaction of the Whole World, and his own Conscience, to declare what he knew concerning him; but he, with a dogged and surly Carriage, told the People, he was not obliged to confess to them; yet immediately before his Death, said he knew nothing of his Master's Death, nor what was become of him, but they might hereafter possibly hear.

The world certainly did hear what had befallen Harrison, for he re-appeared two years after the execution, on 6 August 1662, and had an amazing explanation for his disappearance. This is the story that he told Sir Thomas Overbury, who now had an even keener interest in the affair.

On his return to Campden, after collecting the rents at Charringworth, Harrison found his way blocked by a horseman. After a brief scuffle in which he had tried valiantly to defend himself with his 'little cane' against the sword wielded by the stranger, he was overpowered when two more men came to the aid of the one on horseback. One of them ran a sword through the steward's thigh and, helpless on the ground, Harrison thought that he was being robbed for the money that he carried. Much to his surprise he was hauled to his feet and mounted behind the horseman, his hands being fastened by handcuffs around his waist. They rode for a long time through the night, pausing at a stone-pit where first they took Harrison's money from him, then gave it back plus a great deal more which filled all his pockets. They rode on through the next day until they came to a lonely house on a heath where they dismounted and Harrison was carried inside. By this time he was almost unconscious with pain from the wound in his thigh. The woman of the house, distressed by his condition, gave him broth and 'strong waters' which, with a night's sleep, probably saved his life. They rode for two more days, at last arriving at Deal where they met another mysterious stranger. Harrison's captor fell into discussion with this man and he heard the sum of seven pounds mentioned. Shortly afterwards he was carried aboard a boat where his wounds were dressed and where he remained about six weeks, in company with several other wretches 'in the same condition'. Whether by accident or design the ship was met by three Turkish ships who took off the prisoners to sell them in the slave markets of their native land. Harrison, having said that he had 'some Skill at Physick' was bought by 'a grave Physician of Eighty-seven Years of Age, who lived near to *Smyrna*, who had formerly been in England, and knew *Crowland* in *Lincolnshire*, which he preferred before all other places in England'. He was employed in looking after the distillation room and, as a reward for good work, was given a silver bowl by his master. After a year and three quarters the physician fell ill and having told Harrison that he would have to fend for himself, died. The steward used the silver bowl to bribe a seaman to allow him to stow away on an English ship bound for Lisbon and after a hazardous journey arrived back at Campden.

Harrison's reappearance was widely publicised. A ballad and pamphlet were printed in London telling of the extraordinary events which were usually attributed to witchcraft:

You see how far a Witch's power extends
When as to wickedness her mind she bends,
Great is her Malice, yet can God restrain her,
And at his pleasure let her loose or chain her.
If God had let her work her utmost spight
No doubt she would have killed the man outright,
But he is saved and she for all her malice,
Was very justly hang'd upon the Gallows.

The witch, the widow Perry, is supposed to have used magic to transport Harrison, thrown into the stone-pit by the robbers and left for dead, on to a rock off the coast of Turkey. From there he was rescued and sold as a slave. The pamphlet, published in 1662, also puts the blame on Mrs Perry for his strange arrival in Turkey, but both ballad and pamphlet mention other details which are confirmed in the account given by Harrison later to Sir Thomas Overbury. The Bodleian Library, Oxford, holds copies of both from the collection of Anthony Wood, an assiduous student of local history who lived at Oxford at this time. He also acquired a copy of Harrison's testimony to Sir Thomas Overbury and to this is attached the following handwritten comment:

John Perry hung in chains on the same gallows. Richard and Joan Perry were after execution taken down and buried under the gallows. Three days after a gentle-woman pretending to understand witches hired a man to dig up the grave which was opened but the horse, starting at the sight of the body in the grave, ran away under the gallows and her head hitting against John's feet struck her off from the horse into the grave.

After Harrison's return John was taken down and buried and Harrison's wife soon after (being a snotty covetous presbyterian) hung herself in her own house – why, the reader is to judge.

Possibly the woman was after the 'Hand of Glory'. There was a belief in many parts of Europe and even in Mexico that the hand of a man executed for murder had, if prepared in the correct way with ingredients such as Lapland sesame, virgin wax, and the fat of a hanged man, the magical property of keeping people asleep while the candle clutched in the dead fingers remained alight. In *Thalabra* Southey wrote of the Hand of Glory:

. . . And from his wallet drew a human hand
Shrivelled and dry and black.
And fitting, as he spoke
A taper in his hold,
Pursued, 'A murderer on this stake had died;
I drove the vultures from his limbs, and kept
The hand that did the murder, and drew up
The tendon-strings to close its grasp.
And in the sun and wind
Parched it, nine weeks exposed.
The taper . . . but not here the place to impart,
Nor hast thou undergone the rites
That fit thee to partake the mystery.'

Only by using milk to quench the flame of the candle could the spell be broken. Naturally the Hand was much prized by criminals.

Another local writer of Queen Anne's time elaborated on the death of Harrison's wife:

Mr Harrison's wife fell into a deep melancholy and at last hanged herself after the return of her husband; after her death there was found a letter in her scrutore which she had received from her husband, dated before the execution of Joan and her two sons. There was a report that Joan had bewitched a woman that lay bedridden several years who upon her execution got up and recovered her former state of health.

There is also an amusing note by Wood on the reaction of the judge who had sentenced the Perrys:

Upon Harrison's return to London, Sir R. Hyde was at Gloucester in his circuit and one that had seen H. there brought the news to Gloucester, which coming to the hearinge of Hyde he became somewhat passionate and commanding his servant to call the messenger, chid him for bringing false news and commanded the jailer to commit him to prison.

It is remarkable that after his miraculous arrival back in Campden Harrison lived out the rest of his days as a citizen respected by the community. The accounts of the Grammar School show that he continued to serve as a Governor of the school (an office he had held before his disappearance) until 1672, when he was well over eighty. He died soon after. His story placed great demands on even the most credulous observer. Most importantly, who would go to such a great amount of trouble to sell an old man of seventy into slavery? If robbery was the motive for ambushing him, then why was he kept alive? Was the letter to his wife the malicious invention of an enemy or rival, or merely later gossip? Could such a man have knowingly allowed three innocent people to be hanged?

A great many solutions have been put forward to explain the 'Wonder'. Some dwell on John Perry's passionate need to confess to a murder that was never committed. John Masefield explored this theme in his play on the subject. Other writers emphasise the political uncertainties of the age and speculate on the possibilities of Harrison being a precursor of James Bond. A few prefer to believe that Harrison thought himself bewitched by Joan Perry and devised an elaborate ploy to rid himself of her spell. Hugh Ross Williamson has written a novel[1] which incorporates the witchcraft theory plus a more factual account (in *Historical Mysteries*) which favours Harrison working for the Royalist secret service. In researching his account Williamson found a letter sent by hand from Algiers to Lady Juliana in which her son, the third Viscount Campden, asks for money. He thanks her for her letter received 'by hand of Harrison, oure good servant, who returneth forthwithe, and as I will later'. If Harrison had been working for the King before the Restoration why did he choose to go into hiding after Charles came to the throne? His secret activities must have had to be kept from his wife, the 'snotty covetous presbyterian'. Was John Perry also involved, and

---

[1] *The Silver Bowl*, published 1948, reprinted 1975. This is an intricate, meandering historical romance derived from the story of the Campden Wonder. The Bowl has immense magical power associated with black magic. The story begins fifty years before the events narrated above took place. Baptist Hicks, the builder of Campden House, is given the task of stealing the Silver Bowl from Turkey so that the premier witch of England can use it to cast a spell on Lord Rochester, favourite of King James. He delegates the task to his young protégé William Harrison, who, like Hicks, is an initiate of the Dark Arts. Harrison returns to Campden with the Bowl and is generously rewarded. He becomes Devil of the local coven and in the course of one of their orgies exercises his rights over Joan Perry. The outcome of this is that John Perry is Harrison's natural son. By chance the Silver Bowl ends up forgotten in the house of Thomas Overbury. It is eventually discovered by Overbury who many years later shows it to Harrison, who recognises it and remembers its fearsome magical properties.

Meanwhile an Englishman, Wrenshaw, is employed by a Turkish magician to find the Bowl. After consultation with the Arch-Priest of England Harrison buries the Bowl at Seven Wells. Wrenshaw traces the Bowl to Harrison. The burglary at Campden House is an attempt to discover whether the bowl is hidden there. His Turkish servants later attempt to kidnap John Perry in order to extract the secret of the whereabouts of the Bowl by torture. These two incidents alarm Harrison. He decides to return it to its rightful place at Smyrna, but before he can do so Wrenshaw ambushes him and carries him off, with the precious Bowl, to his master in Turkey. This 'aged physician' intends to use the Bowl to give him the elixir of eternal youth. However, he is unsuccessful in this and dies two years after Harrison's capture. The latter is left with a replica of the Bowl and he sells this in order to secure his passage to England.

Back home he finds that his son, John Perry, has been hung for a crime that was never committed. None of the Perrys could speak of the real fate of Harrison because to do so would implicate all of the coven. *The Silver Bowl* is fascinating for the ingenious solutions that Williamson offers for many of the problems of the story, though in the end the feeling is that the bones of the story are best left bare of explanation.

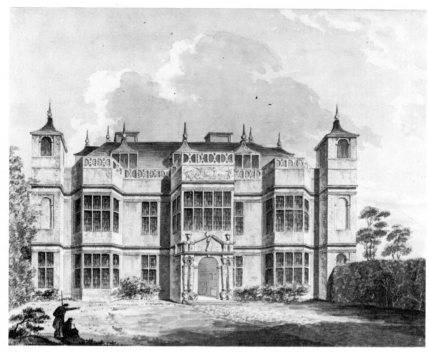

Campden House

if so, did his loyalty make him suffer on the gallows together with his mother and brother who were also innocent? There is just one other possibility. Edward, Harrison's son, was ambitious, impatiently waiting for his father to retire or die so that he could succeed him as steward. Did he steal the money from Campden House in order to pay to have his father put out of the way (though not killed)? It would certainly have been in character for he was disliked in the village for his meanness and bullying nature. The story of the Campden Wonder remains one of the most intriguing of all historical enigmas.

The Most Haunted Village – Prestbury

Prestbury – a phantom rider often passes this cottage

The Most Haunted Village – Prestbury

Prestbury is a village whose character has altered drastically in the last fifty years. Modern transport enables people to live in peaceful surroundings here and work in Cheltenham, only four miles away. Thus it has become a village of old cottages and modern bungalows, the latter carefully segregated into 'closes' of their own in an attempt to preserve the original 'olde worlde' atmosphere of the place. One would think that these recent

Prestbury church

Reform Cottage

changes might be resented by the numerous ghosts but it seems that the pattern of their hauntings continues in the same way today as it did in the past.

In medieval times the land here was divided between the Bishopric of Hereford and the monks of Llanthony Priory. The latter provided the parish priest, while the Bishop established a hunting-lodge at Prestbury and entertained guests on a lavish scale. At a Christmas banquet in 1289 he provided 500 different dishes. Not surprisingly in view of this both the monks from Llanthony and the village to whom they ministered resented the Bishop's autocratic use of the district's resources.

Perhaps an ancient grievance between the two sets of clergy causes the thrice-yearly appearance of the Black Abbot. His hooded figure may be seen at Easter, Christmas, and on All Saints' Day. His walk starts in the church, continues through the churchyard, and ends at Reform Cottage close by. This is a weather-boarded cottage dating from the sixteenth century that stands on Deep Street. A long front garden separates it from this busy thoroughfare and the site of the garden is supposed to have been the burial-ground of the monks who came to Prestbury from Llanthony. On each of the three church festivals footsteps are heard approaching the cottage. There is a brief pause as though the person is hesitating before knocking at the door and then mysterious sounds come from the attic – more footsteps, and the sounds of things being knocked over, though later investigation always reveals everything in its rightful place. At the time of my visit to Prestbury the cottage was up for sale (spring 1979); it will be interesting to hear if the phenomenon continues. A secret passageway is supposed to link the cottage with the church, but even more mysterious are the concealed stone steps in the hillside overlooking the village which probably once led to a hermit's cave high in a limestone cliff.

Prestbury's most famous ghost is the cavalier on horseback who is frequently heard galloping through the Burgage and Mill Lane (there are also reports of him riding down Shaw Green and Bow Bridge Lanes). During the Civil War the inhabitants of Prestbury House supported the Cromwellian cause and operated a primitive roadblock (a rope stretched across the road) opposite their house. One night they were successful in dismounting a Royalist dispatch rider who was caught and executed on the spot. This is the incident that the ghostly ride commemorates. Confusingly, another ghost on horseback haunts the same locality. He is a knight in armour who pauses to salute before galloping away (in contrast to the cavalier whose headlong flight always ends abruptly).

Among the lesser-known ghosts of Prestbury is the old lady dressed in ancient clothes who peers into the windows of buildings in the main street. She disappears by the Almshouses put up by Ann Goodrich in 1720. A phantom shepherd, complete with ghostly sheep, was seen in Swindon Lane on a foggy autumn night in 1975. Herdsmen often have difficulty in driving their flocks past the Plough Inn, Mill Street. Dogs also freeze at this point: their hackles rise and they show the whites of their eyes – a sure sign of acute distress in a dog. Horses too sense evil here yet no one can account for it unless it has something to do with an apparition known as Mrs Preece's Ghost which also haunts Mill Lane. This has been described as a white misty form which glides across the fields towards the lane. When it reaches the wall it seems to hesitate for a moment and then vanishes.

Better known is the cultured ghost of Sundial Cottage who is heard playing the spinet. This is supposed to have been a Professor of Music who taught pupils in the room from which the sounds emanate.

Out towards the Racecourse is a converted coach-house known as Walnut Cottage. This is haunted by 'Old Moses', a genial ghost who, when an owner of the cottage challenged him one day in the dining-room, answered: 'Here's Old Moses! You see I likes to look in sometimes.' Opinions differ as to who Old Moses was. He may have been a somewhat villainous racehorse trainer who was 'a rough rider with various horse-people about the place', though he could also have been a groom who lived here in the eighteenth century. His favourite haunt was the dining-room and once when the owner of the cottage said vehemently at dinner that he could never believe in ghosts a large mirror inexplicably fell from the wall.

Prestbury's connections with racing are very strong, the village being situated so close to the racecourse. One of the most famous of all jockeys was born in a cottage in the village where a plaque reads: 'This is the house where Fred Archer, the famous jockey, once lived and ate his earliest porridge.' However, his ghost never materialises here, but, more suitably perhaps, haunts Newmarket Heath, the scene of many of his triumphs. The sudden appearance of his ghost has been blamed for many strange mishaps at the Suffolk racecourse.

The only malevolent ghost in Prestbury is the one that is said to haunt Cleeve Corner, a rambling old house situated close to the church. Part of it once accommodated the monks that looked

after the interests of Llanthony Priory in the district before the Reformation. A horrible murder is supposed to have been committed in one of the bedrooms where a young bride was strangled in her bed by a thief who made off with the marriage gifts and her jewellery (another version says that her husband murdered her for the dowry). Those who try to sleep in this room now run the risk of being woken up in the middle of the night with the sense of evil invading the room. An unearthly light shines through the window and the air turns cold and clammy. Suddenly a terrible pressure is felt on the throat and this grows tighter and tighter only to be relaxed if the victim can gasp out a prayer. Then the unseen hands are taken away. Fortunately none of the other ghosts of the village are harmful so that Prestbury can safely claim to be the ghost-hunter's Mecca of the Cotswolds.

The Ghosts of Warwick and the East

A dungeon at Warwick Castle

The Ghosts of Warwick and the East

Warwick stands just inside the vague boundaries of the 'Cotswold Country' and, as the forbidding walls of its great castle suggest, it is a town where momentous events of history were shaped. Many of the earls of Warwick who owned the castle were rich and powerful, even rivalling the monarch in medieval times: but for all their wealth and influence they could still occasionally be troubled by 'things supernatural'.

Moll Bloxham was a dairymaid at the castle in the fifteenth century, famous locally for the potency of her spells. She enjoyed many illegal 'perks' at the expense of the Earl of Warwick, and also cheated the townspeople who bought butter and cheese from the castle dairy. For a long time her customers put up with short weights for fear of being bewitched but at last her fellow servants told the Earl of her dishonesty, and he brought Moll before him and dismissed her immediately, perhaps refraining from sending her to one of his dungeons because he too was frightened of her powers.

Moll flew into a terrible rage and took herself off to a tiny room at the top of the Beauchamp Tower where she set about making the most fearful potions directed against her former employer. The Earl enlisted the help of the Church to overcome these and three priests were sent up the winding stairs to confront Moll, each being armed with the traditional bell, book, and candle. When her door was broken down a great black 'Hell-hound' faced them, its eyes blazing red and its lips drawn back to reveal demoniac fangs. Instead of attacking the priests it recoiled from their instruments of exorcism, but then rushed past them and threw itself over the battlements and into the river far below. Since there was no sign of Moll in the room it was assumed that she had taken the form of this fearsome hound who met his match in the three priests. Her ghost still visits the castle occasionally, though her spirit is usually imprisoned in the tumultuous waters of the weir.

Visitors to the castle are shown a 'Bogey Room' which is supposed to be haunted by a seventeenth-century owner, Sir Fulke Greville. He was murdered in this room by his servant, Heywood, who was enraged at discovering that he was left out of his master's will. Many people feel the atmosphere in this chamber strange, and my own experience there may confirm this. I was working at the castle (taking photographs) during a 'winter of discontent' when power cuts would black out town and country without notice. One of these cuts occurred at dusk and as I walked through the 'Bogey Room' in the half-light I saw an unnatural miasmic mist in front of me at face-level. It vaguely resembled the smoke from a cigarette but was odourless and struck the face with a distinct chill. Of course, this may be

Warwick Castle

dismissed as auto-suggestion as I knew of the room's reputation, but to me it remains a disturbing and inexplicable experience.

In Castle Street below the walls of the castle is the Doll Museum, situated in a beautiful half-timbered house occupied in Elizabethan times by Thomas Oken, a wealthy merchant and generous benefactor to the town. His footsteps are still to be heard on the stairs late at night, always descending, and always ending on the last step but one. The explanation for this is that the height of the ceilings has been raised by lowering the floor level – thus the steps would have stopped at ground level at the time when Oken lived.

Burton Dassett lies on the Banbury road out of Warwick, just within the boundaries of Warwickshire. With neighbouring Fenny Compton and the hamlet of Northend in between, the village was famous for its 'Jenny Burn Tail', the local name for Will o' the Wisps, Jack o' Lanterns, or Jenny Pinketts. This phenomenon is usually attributed to the spontaneous com-bustion of marsh gas rising up from vegetation submerged and rotting in marshy ground. The unearthly light flits across treacherous ground and was often blamed for leading travellers to disaster. A local journalist who investigated Jenny in 1920 (in February when one would be particularly surprised to discover her, as it is the heat of a summer's day that usually causes her appearance in the evening) reported that he spotted the light from a mile away and that it was considerably brighter than a car headlamp. This is not surprising, though, since at that time many vehicles still used carbide lamps. 'Its radiance was such that the sky was faintly illumined for several miles, and it was easy to understand the effect which such a glow would produce when seen close at hand.... The light appeared to be travelling towards Fenny Compton and, as usual, by the time it reached a woodland tract known locally as Bottom Cover, it faded from view. The fact that the light has invariably been seen to travel in this direction is a somewhat curious circumstance, but at any rate it affords confirmation of the theory that the agglomeration of gas obeys a natural impulse and follows a natural course.'

The writer then draws a distinction between this light and the common bogland 'Will o' the Wisp'. It differs from this 'alike in size and steadiness . . . the most remarkable feature of the display is the form and intensity of the glow'. Although he is at pains to dismiss any suspicion of the supernatural in his explanation, the account brings to mind the sighting of an UFO rather than a gentle 'Jenny Burn Tail'. It would seem to be highly unlikely that a patch of methane gas would always follow the same path, least of all in the coldest month of the year.

Compton Wynyates is the epitome of an old English manor house; overlooked by wooded hills, its brick walls reflect an aura of history and romance. It would be strange if such a house did not have its haunted rooms. One was discovered when a child fell against some panelling. A secret door swung open to reveal a skeleton lying by an overturned table. Its clothing was perfectly preserved and dated from the seventeenth century. Presumably the unfortunate gentleman had been locked into the secret room and then some misfortune had befallen the person who had concealed him there. Terrible moans and shuffling footsteps emanate from this part of the house. Another room has a window that can never be fastened, and strange noises are heard from it.

As we have seen, Brailes was famous for its witches. One of

Compton Wynyates

89

them, Granny or Nancy Austin, still appears on New Year's Eve. She thoroughly frightened a member of the Home Guard on patrol in 1943 when her dark legless shape floated past him. When he told his colleagues they accepted his story in a matter-of-fact way as though it would surprise them *not* to see Granny at that place on the last evening of the year.

Near Stretton-on-Fosse two men, walking back to the village after an evening with their girl friends, came across a hare that persisted in running in circles around their legs. Exasperated, they at last drove it off with kicks and blows from their sticks. As soon as it disappeared the hedgerow burst into flames. Terrified, the two men ran the rest of the way home. When they returned to the scene the next day they found the hedge intact.

The hare is held to be a mystical animal throughout England. Two beliefs unique to Warwickshire concern goats and peacocks.

Even in the last century few people in the county would keep goats; they thought them unlucky animals as they had to pay regular visits to the Devil to have their beards combed. If one brought a peacock's feather indoors disaster invariably followed. They had been the doorkeepers to Paradise until one day they let in the Devil by mistake. Thereafter they were banished from 'the riches of bliss' and hence their anguished cries.

In his selections from the Carter Manuscripts, Percy Manning included the following story of an unfortunate family who were plagued by a ghost.

Thomas Hall, blacksmith, and Ann his wife, lived at Little Tew about fifty years ago (1850). While there, they were troubled with supernatural visits. No ghosts were seen, but noises of different kinds were heard. Sometimes they would be sitting at meals, when there would be a sound as of a cock crowing very loudly; then the dishes, etc., in the cupboard would sound as if they were being smashed. At last Hall and his wife left Little Tew, and went to Hook Norton, where he set up in business; but the same noises were heard here. Mrs Bench, mother of Mrs Hall, told how when she went to bed there was a noise under her head in the pillow, as if someone were groaning. She actually struck the pillow with a pen-knife, and blood appeared on it. The Halls left Hook Norton and came to Enstone, where they again set up a smithy; but here the noises were worse than ever. Jeffries (a neighbour who related these events to Carter) says that he often went into the blacksmith's shop to help Hall, and that when he was striking the iron, it seemed as though someone took hold of the handle of the hammer and made him miss his stroke. Once, when he was talking to the Halls in their sitting-room, the fire-irons suddenly left their places and walked across the room, whereupon Jeffries bolted. Another time, when Mrs Hall was laying the table for dinner, a voice asked for a plate as well, and Mrs Hall said that she was obliged to put one, or there would be no peace. Jeffries often heard the plates and dishes rattling as though they were all coming down together. Once he was in the house talking to Hall when

there was a bang as if a gun had been fired, and a bullet came through the door and hit the table. No hole was to be seen in the door. Hall and his wife have been dead some years, and no noises are now heard in Enstone. Mrs Jeffries says that Mrs Hall was always very strange, but she liked her as a neighbour.

Chipping Norton has the ghost of a former vicar who was an active leader of the 1549 rebellion and was subsequently hung from his own church tower. Just to the south on the A361 is the hamlet of Puddlicote. 'Gran' was an old recluse who lived in a cave in a nearby quarry where she had hidden a hoard of gold sovereigns. Her ghost, in the form of a 'white lady', is supposed to haunt the road junction here.

Deddington is one of the easternmost outposts of the Cotswolds. Its vicarage saw brief supernatural activity after the death of the Rev. Maurice Frost in 1961. He was a great bibliophile and also had a wonderful collection of antique clocks. His books were moved about and the clocks wound up by themselves until all of his effects were moved from the house. 'The Paddocks', in the same village, also has the reputation of being haunted. Two girls sharing a room in the house one Christmas were terrified to hear the sounds of footsteps approaching their beds. Before they fled they glimpsed a pair of old-fashioned boots that they assumed had made the noise. These had vanished when they returned to the room in the morning. A man in a dark suit also haunts the house, which has had many tragic episodes in its history: a groom was kicked to death in the stables and a suicide took place in the grounds.

The Chipping Norton to Deddington road is haunted by a strange 'elemental force' which, Christina Hole wrote in 1954, causes cyclists to dismount and horses to bolt. This phenomenon is most likely to be encountered at Hempton. The village of Kirtlington boasts a ghost that was only laid with the greatest difficulty in a pond which, should it ever run dry, will again release the spirit of wicked Sir James Dashwood, who died in 1779.

Before leaving this area the tale of the only ghost to be called as a witness in a court of law must be told. It comes from

Ackermann's 'Repository', November 1820, and was reprinted in the *Weekly Post* in 1907.

A Warwickshire farmer was murdered as he returned from Southam market. Probably the perpetrator of the crime would never have been discovered but for a false move on his part. On the morning following the commission of the crime a man waited upon the widow and told her that as he lay awake in bed her husband's ghost had appeared to him, and after showing him several stab wounds on his body, had informed him that he was murdered by a certain person, and his corpse thrown into a marl-pit, the situation of which he described. This led to the marl-pit being examined and the body was discovered and the wounds found to be in the exact places spoken of by the 'ghost'. He was regarded as a particularly veracious ghost and on his testimony the person named was arrested and committed to the Warwick Assizes, the judge of which happened to be Lord Chief Justice Raymond. The jury, after hearing the evidence, were inclined to convict the prisoner, but his lordship interposed, remarking that he did not put any credit in the pretended ghost story since the prisoner was a man of unblemished reputation, and no ill-feeling had ever existed between himself and the deceased. He added that he knew of no law which admitted the evidence of a ghost, and if any did the ghost had better appear. The crier was thereupon ordered to summon the ghost, which he did in the orthodox manner three times, but there was no response, whereupon the Lord Chief Justice directed the acquittal of the accused, which was done by the jury. The accuser of the prisoner was arrested by order of the judge, and upon his house being searched by the parish constables such strong evidences of his connection with the murder were discovered that he made a full confession. He was sent for trial at the following assizes where he was convicted, and a few days later paid the penalty for his crime with his life.

Around Stratford

Stratford-upon-Avon Churchyard

Around Stratford

'Ghost stories are not very common in the neighbourhood of Stratford-upon-Avon', wrote J. Harvey Bloom in 1929, 'and very few of those told have any interest.' It is one of the sad truths of ghost-hunting that places which one would expect to have the perfect atmosphere for a haunting turn out to be ghost-free. As is apparent in this book, many of the most famous picture-book villages of the Cotswolds fail even to produce a wraith with a pedigree (viz. a written account of appearances and an explanation for them if possible), let alone a decent ghost. In fact many of the best stories come from places on the periphery of the area. So it is with Stratford: only the ghosts of the Walton Hall Hotel and Clopton House save it from complete neglect.

A white horse gallops across the lawns in front of the hotel on 9 October at five-yearly intervals – it leaves no hoofprints. A young man is said to haunt Room 117 and has also been seen in the bar and library. He has even played with the proprietor's children. Clothes put away tidily in the wardrobe in 117 have later been found in disarray on the floor of the room. Dogs refuse to enter this room. The story that explains the presence of this ghost has echoes of a famous Scottish legend – that of the monster of Glamis. The wife of an owner of the house was caught by her husband *in flagrante delicto* with a prince of the realm. The husband fired shots after the fleeing figure of the prince, who was mounted on a large white horse, but only succeeded in hitting the latter. A short time later his wife gave birth to a son who turned out to be mentally deranged and given to violent fits. He was kept locked in a barred room in the west wing of the house until an early death ended his unhappy life.

This story comes from Roy Palmer's *Folklore of Warwickshire* which also quotes a *Stratford Herald* report of ghosts in another hotel close to Stratford – Salford Hall, near Bidford. In this case it is Room 5 which is haunted. A nun was found dead in this room on the same night that her sister was stabbed to death in Buckinghamshire.

After William Shakespeare, the greatest benefactor to Stratford-upon-Avon must be the Clopton family. Hugh Clopton was Lord Mayor of London in the reign of Henry VII and built the

Clopton House

'great and sumptuose bridge' over the Avon to the east of the medieval town. This was the first stone bridge to span the river and replaced a hazardous timber structure that was swept away in times of flood. The family were extremely wealthy merchants and built an imposing home to the north of the town, close to the Welcombe Hotel.

However, for all their riches the Cloptons suffered many tragedies through the ages. In the time of Charles II the exquisite young daughter of the house, Charlotte, was struck down with the Plague, which was then relaxing its grip on London but spreading its tentacles into the countryside. The beautiful girl was loved by all the household, both for her looks and for her sweet nature, but when she was pronounced to be dead by the physician her body was hastily interred in the family vault in Holy Trinity Church to prevent the infection from spreading further. But her mother was stricken already and also died within a couple of days. She too was quickly borne off to the church, and when the vault was re-opened the dim light of the bearers' lanterns showed that poor Charlotte had been buried alive. She had succeeded in escaping from her coffin and her body in its shroud was lying against the wall of the crypt. In her last agony she had bitten deep into her flesh in an attempt to relieve the torments of hunger and thirst. Her ghost acts out this terrible experience as she glides through the rooms of Clopton House.

A well at the back of the house attracts the restless spirit of another member of the family, Margaret Clopton. She threw herself into the well and drowned after an unhappy love affair three centuries ago. Overlooking the chapel there is a lonely garret where bloodstains can still be seen on the floor – a grim reminder of a horrible murder that once took place in the room. The murderer, or possibly his victim, occasionally revisits the scene.

At Coughton Court near Alcester, the home of the Throckmorton family, there is a persistent ghost which even defied Sir Robert Throckmorton's determined attempts to get rid of it in the late eighteenth century. He made many alterations to the house in the course of which a rusty sword was found beneath the floorboards of a small room in the south-west turret – a place particularly favoured by the ghost. The sword was claimed to be that of Sir Francis Smith who bravely rescued the King's Standard at the Battle of Edgehill. For all Sir Robert's efforts, unearthly footsteps continue to be heard coming down the main staircase, turning into the drawing-room, and then climbing to the south-west turret. Sometimes faint breathing and the rustle of clothing is also heard.

This part of Warwickshire was once exceptionally well-endowed with deer-parks which may well account for a strange figure, part beast, part human, which haunted the lanes at night and kept villagers at home after nightfall. Alscot and Wimpstone both have stories of this frightening apparition, which Bloom believed was in reality a white-face doe escaped from Alscot or

Coughton Court

Ragley Park. Many years ago a skeleton was found in the latter grounds. It was obviously that of a lady for her beautiful dress was preserved and she wore a wonderful array of jewellery. The ghost of this creature, dressed in white, is still seen close to the spot where the remains were found, though no one knows who she was or how she died.

In the *Gentleman's Magazine*, July 1855, there appeared the following account of a haunting at Beoley, the northernmost village of our area, which includes a novel way of laying a ghost:

At Beoley, about half a century ago, the ghost of a reputed murderer managed to keep undisputed possession of a certain house, until a conclave of the clergy chained him to the bed of the Red Sea for fifty years. When that term was expired the ghost re-appeared (two or three years ago), and more than ever frightened the natives of the said house, slamming the doors, and racing through the ceilings. The inmates, however, took heart and chased him by stamping on the floor, from one room to another, under the impression that, could they once drive him to a trap-door opening into the cheese-room (for which, if the ghost happens to be a rat, he has a very natural *penchant*), he would disappear for a season. The beadle of the parish, who also combined with that office the scarcely less important one of pig-sticker, declared to the writer that he dared not go by the house in the morning till the sun was up. (It was an ancient superstition that evil spirits flew away at cock-crowing.)

Ebrington, close to Chipping Campden, lacks a ghost but under its alternative derisory name, Yubberton, has the reputation of being the 'silly village' of the Cotswolds. Many stories are told to illustrate the stupidity of the villagers. They once put manure round the walls of the church in an attempt to make it grow to rival Campden church. When the muck dried out and shrank leaving a brown stain on the walls they were encouraged to believe that their idea was working!

Worcester and the North-West

Bretforton

Worcester and the North-West

Evesham takes its name from Eoves, a swineherd employed by Bishop Ecgwin. One day he was deep in the woods of Blakenhurst searching for a lost sow. He found her with her litter by the banks of the Avon and the place was so tranquil and beautiful that he lay down for a time by the river, even though he knew that this part of the wilderness was infamous for its hobgoblins and evil spirits of the woods. The stillness was broken by the sound of wonderful music sung, it seemed, by an ethereal choir. The mist over the water then lifted to reveal the form of a lady of breathtaking beauty, flanked by two handmaidens, all dressed in brilliantly shining garments. This vision grew more and more distinct until Eoves felt that he could touch the very images, yet it dissolved into the hues of the rainbow as suddenly as it had formed. The swineherd hurried back to tell his master of the remarkable experience. Impressed with his sincerity, Ecgwin and two monks visited the site of the vision themselves, walking barefoot and singing psalms on the way. As the Bishop, a little separate from the rest of the party, knelt in prayer, the miraculous sequence was repeated just as Eoves had narrated it, and Ecgwin knew that the Blessed Virgin had led him to this spot so that he could found a church in the wilderness. Thus the Benedictine Abbey was founded, in the year 714.

The last abbot of Evesham was Clement Lichfield who erected the beautiful 110-foot-high bell tower that stands between the two churches of the town in the meadows by the Avon. The tower was completed in 1539, the same year as the dissolution of the abbey. The Abbot is said to have hidden the peal of silver bells in the bed of the river where they may be heard to ring at midnight on Christmas Eve. Other stories say that the bells were hidden at Abbots Morton and also in the woods above Broadway where again they ring out on rare occasions.

Evesham

During the reign of Edward II St Catherine Audley wandered through Worcestershire helping the poor and nursing the sick. She had a vision that told her not to rest until she came to a town where the bells rang of their own accord. The Devil is supposed to have been so angry at the good that she was doing that he stole her horse and pony, hiding them in Sapey brook. However, Catharine prayed that wherever they went their tracks would be left for all to see and so the hoofprints may still be seen today indelibly etched into the rocky bed of the stream.

The Evesham road out of Broadway passes close to a field that was the scene of a tragic episode two centuries ago. Ephraim Rolfe was a simple-minded young boy who earned a meagre living as a bird-scarer. For all his lack of wits he was well-loved in the village for his kindness to children and uncanny understanding of animals. Ephraim was shot dead by the squire who thought him a poacher. On wild nights when the moon occasionally sends flashes of eerie light through the clouds he can still be seen standing in the fields – a skeletal scarecrow.

The local name for a ghost in this district is 'spot-loggin', which seems to have derived from the much-haunted village of Bretforton. There is supposed to be a monument in the church to Robert Loggin, Gent., who died in 1688 (though today it is not readily visible). It is said that a lady of the family was given to patching her face with beauty-spots. Perhaps it is this unhappy creature who haunts the fields around the church, her head tucked beneath her arm in exemplary style. There is also a spectral funeral procession to be seen in Bretforton churchyard which comes from Weston Subedge. A past vicar's recipe for ridding a house of ghosts must have been equally effective against insects and other vermin:

Lay half a pound of Brimstone in an iron dish, supported
by a pair of tongs over a bucket of water; the fireplace and
all openings to be closed, a shovelful of burning coal put
on the brimstone, the door quickly shut and the room kept
closed for six hours. This is one of the best ways of laying a
ghost.

A phantom coach is driven across ditches and through hedges by a headless coachman from Littleton towards Bretforton, perhaps tracing the path of a trackway that vanished long ago. A particularly alarming 'spot-loggin' lurks at Aldington, in the little lane that runs by the orchard of the Lodge (the account dates from 1907 so possibly both lane and orchard have now vanished).

In 1899 a disquieting account came from Cropthorne (though the same ghost was also claimed for Hinton, where the Old Manor House was supposed to be the house concerned; here the ghost became so persistent that part of the building had to be pulled down). This is the original account:

At Cropthorne in Gloucestershire, a beautiful place with
good shooting stands vacant because successive owners
have found it impossible to keep any servants there. A
booted 'something' enters at the front door, crosses the
hall, ascends the stairs and proceeds to an attic, where it
apparently sits down and casts off first one boot and then
the other. The latest lessees of this place, who are alive
now, have stood on the stairs and heard the footsteps pass
between them; and the dogs (one a mastiff) have remained

paralysed with terror, their hair literally standing on end.

Another phantom coach haunts the countryside between Lenchwick and Evesham. A driveway once linked Old Lenchwick Manor House to the main road and here:

> ... on certain nights a spectral coach was, or, it may be, is still, seen; the horses breathed forth fire, flames flashed from their eyes and from the coachman's whip. Within sat the figure of a man with a red mark around his neck as though he had been beheaded. This fearful equipage dashed down the road until it reached the site of Evesham Abbey where it instantly disappeared. Now my recent research has revealed in a most interesting way some badly-damaged membranes of parchment at the Public Record Office, and from which it appears that Gabriel Bigge, that 'miles ... fortis et intrepidus', as he is styled on his tablet on the south wall of the chancel in Norton Church, was attacked on May 6, 1615, in Evesham by one John Wybon, a labourer, who struck him on the head with a long pike which he held in both hands. This attack, the result of a quarrel, proved fatal, and Gabriel Bigge was buried at Norton four days later.

This account (taken from the *Evesham Journal*, November 1919) fails to tell of the fate of the murderer, but it seems to me that the red mark on the neck of the ghost in the carriage must be that of the hangman's noose.

At Church Lench there was a house, described as being like the Poet's Birthplace at Stratford, which for many years was the headquarters of a gang of criminals – highwaymen, thieves and cut-throats. Many dreadful deeds were committed there, including more than one murder, and when part of the building was pulled down much later (to make way for the schools) human bones were found buried into the foundations. A black servant who vanished from the village is said to have been killed there because he threatened to expose the villains to justice. Naturally the house subsequently harboured several ghosts and everyone in the district knew it as 'the haunted house'. It was difficult to find tenants for it as even people usually insensitive to psychic disturbances were frightened by the bumps and screams that they encountered in this place. Strange lights glowed on walls and a figure bearing a candle that cast no shadow was seen to float through rooms. Loud noises used to come from the upper rooms as though large objects were being rolled across the floor.

Norgrove Hall, at Feckenham, was once one of the grandest houses of the county, the home of the Cook family. They even entertained royal hunting parties. After one of these the host returned with his guests to the Hall to find dinner unprepared. Enraged by this he beheaded the cook with one of his own kitchen knives. He then fled the country and so escaped having to pay the penalty for his deed which is commemorated by a 'bloody hand' in the family's coat of arms.

Huddington Court is haunted by the ghost of Lady de Winter. Headless, she walks round the moat and up the avenue of oaks – a favourite walk with her husband who was executed for his part in the Gunpowder Plot. She appears each year on the anniversary of his execution.

Hindlip Hall was another beautiful Worcestershire house with connections with the Plot. Like Huddington it contained 'priests' holes' and secret passages. Thomas Hobbingdon, who was the owner of Hindlip at the time of Guy Fawkes, was condemned to death for helping the Papist cause but was reprieved when his wife wrote a letter that betrayed the conspiracy. He returned to live at Hindlip where priests continued to be sheltered, as this story, from *Notes & Queries*, relates:

Oldcorn, Hobbingdon's father confessor, who is described by some Catholic writers as the apostle of Worcestershire, together with Gornet, another Catholic priest, was hid in one of the secret rooms in the north chimney for a long time. The dangers they were exposed to, and their miraculous escapes, were described as inconceivable. The circumstances were very extraordinary attending the search after these two priests in this retreat, and the miracles that are said to have ensued. Tradition states that Lady Hobbingdon, who by the by was a very pious and good person, could have no peace for the strange sights and noises which were said to be heard in the old Hall. A milk-white calf, with a wreath of white roses around its neck, was said to haunt this place. At last it became so bold that it came up to her ladyship's room in the depth of night on All Saints' Eve, just as the large clock in the Hall struck one, when all the household had retired to rest. It came to her bedside, and seemed to move its head as though it beckoned her ladyship to follow it; she determined to do so; it led her through secret rooms, back staircases, sliding panels, and numerous trap-doors, until it came to the north chimney: it then stopped all on a sudden and dropped a piece of paper, and then vanished. Her ladyship was so struck with fear and amazement that she could scarcely move; at length she picked up the paper, and it contained only one word, 'Search'. She was more puzzled than ever, as she could find nothing, and what was more, she was at a loss to find her way back to her chamber. She stamped her foot with vexation to think how simple she must have been to come here at all, when all at once a large carved oak chimney-piece seemed to give way and move quite out of its place, and she discovered what appeared to be a room in the chimney: what was her horror, when she discovered two human beings actually living in the room, almost in a state of starvation. These two beings were Gornet and Oldcorn in their hiding place. This lady went every night, just as the great clock struck one, to take them food and drink; and for years afterwards this lady and the white calf were seen gliding through the secret places of this mansion on All Saints' Eve. This old mansion was taken down about seventy years ago, and a new one built, now the residence of Sir Henry Allsop, Bart.

Another house on the outskirts of Worcester, Astwood Court, used to have an oak table that bore the imprint of the fingers and hand of a lady ghost who, tired of the lack of response that she got from her appearances, struck the table one resounding blow and disappeared for ever.

Holt Castle, to the north of the city, used to have a lady in black who was particularly fond of frequenting a passageway near the attics. The cellars were occupied by a more dutiful ghost, 'an ill-favoured bird like a raven, which would sometimes pounce upon any person who ventured to approach a cask for drink, and having extinguished the candle with a horrible flapping of wings would leave its victim prostrated with fright. A solution has been given to this legend, however, which would imply a little cunning selfishness on the part of the domestics who had care of the ale and cider depot.' (*Correspondence of Sylvanus Urban*, July 1855.)

The first cathedral at Worcester was put up by St Oswald in 961. There is a story told of its building when a prepared stone was found to be immovable, even resisting the efforts of eighty men. Then someone spotted a grinning imp sitting on top but he easily avoided the attempts of the men to dislodge him. St Oswald was sent for and when he confronted the imp the mischievous spirit vanished as mysteriously as he had come.

About 1041 Worcester was sacked by the Danes. Most of the townspeople saved themselves by fleeing from the city as they saw the sinister black boats of the invaders come up the Severn, but some of the old and infirm were left in the houses and they were mercilessly slaughtered, many being left to burn alive as the buildings were put to the torch. Having loaded their boats with all the valuables that they could steal, the Danes sailed off down the river, but one of their number was greedy. He was struggling to dismantle the Sanctus bell of the Cathedral and was so engrossed with this task that he failed to notice the departure of his colleagues. The monks and townspeople returned to find their city ablaze and the lone Dane at the Cathedral trying to steal its only remaining treasure. They fell upon him and flayed him alive: his skin was tanned and hung on the inside of the great west door of the Cathedral when it was rebuilt, as a warning to the sacrilegious. Remnants of it were still shown to visitors to the Cathedral up to the middle years of the last century when a specimen was sent away for analysis and it was confirmed that the skin was human. Of course the original doors had been replaced long before.

Several legends tell of Cromwell's league with the Devil before the Battle of Worcester on 3 September 1651. This conflict resolved the Civil War and forced Charles II to flee for his life – it was described by the Protector as a 'crowning mercy', though there were many others who regarded it as an infernal judgment.

One account tells how on the morning of the battle Cromwell, accompanied by Lindsey, 'an intimate friend of Cromwell's, the first Captain of his Regiment, and therefore commonly called Colonel Lindsey', rode to a wood close to where his army was encamped. They dismounted and went a little way into the wood where Lindsey was 'seized with horror from some unknown cause' and hung back even though Cromwell called him a faint-hearted fool. However, he saw his general meet with a grave elderly man who carried a roll of parchment which Cromwell took eagerly.

'Said Cromwell loudly, "This is but for seven years, I
was to have had it for one and Twenty, and it must and
shall be so."' But although he attempted to bargain, the
stranger was adamant so that in the end the document
was accepted by Cromwell who, returning to Lindsey,
cried 'with great Joy in his Countenance "Now, Lindsey,
the Battle is our own! I long to be engag'd."'

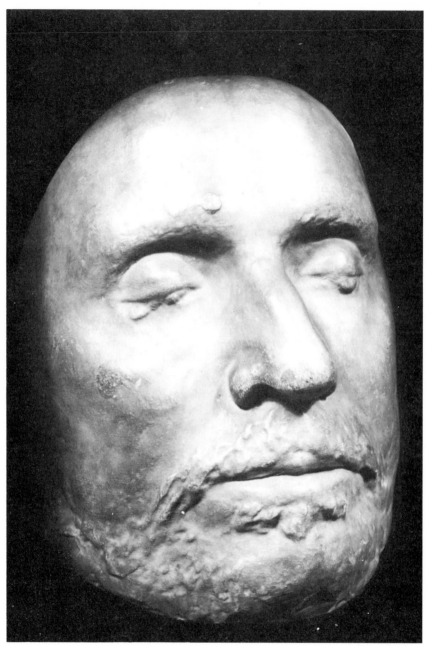

The death-mask of Oliver Cromwell

Lindsey was so upset by this encounter that he abandoned his position after the first charge and fled to Norfolk. There he told his story to a parson friend, Mr Thorowgood, concluding '. . . that Cromwell would certainly die that Day seven Years that the Battel was fought'. The parson made his twelve-year-old son write down Lindsey's account verbatim in his commonplace book. Meanwhile Cromwell had raised a hue and cry after Lindsey, offering a large reward for his capture. Whether this was because he was a witness to the Protector's meeting with the stranger or because he deserted his position is unknown. Nash's famous *History of Worcestershire* mentions the mysterious meeting before the battle but says that it was with a citizen of the city and not with the Devil. However, Cromwell certainly died on the anniversary of the conflict – at 3 p.m. on 3 September 1658. Strangely, Cromwell won the Battle of Dunbar on the same date in 1650.

An article in an ancient edition of the *Evesham Journal* tells a different story:

White Lady's Aston Court was of some antiquity, containing a fine guesten or dining hall; with a moat and drawbridge. This place is chiefly notable for the historical interest attached to it, by being the residence of one Justice Symonds, who entertained Oliver Cromwell on the eve of the battle of Worcester, which took place 3 September 1651. Tradition asserts that Cromwell and Symonds were engaged in deep conversation in the guesten hall, when they were both interrupted by hearing a very strange and unearthly noise proceeding from the chimney, and what was their astonishment in looking up to perceive a figure sitting on the gay-pole or smoke-jack in the large open chimney, the lights were instantly extinguished, and all was perfect darkness. When fresh lights were procured there was a gentleman in black, who by the by, had a cloven foot, sitting between Cromwell and Symonds, who spoke in a very deep and sepulchral voice to Cromwell, and said, 'Tomorrow, at Worcester, the day shall be thine on one condition, on this day seven years I shall claim you as mine.' Cromwell considered for a little while and then said, 'Give me twenty-one or fourteen years.' The gentleman in black stamped his cloven foot impatiently, 'I tell thee in seven years I will claim thee, and not one minute longer. You must decide instantly or it will be too late.' Then the clock struck one. A gentleman in black with a cloven foot, mounted on a coal-black steed, rode in front of Cromwell's forces to Worcester, where they pitched their tents near Perry Road. Immediately the gentleman in black crossed the drawbridge of White Lady's Aston Court, he turned to Symonds and said,

'The last of your race to Satan will be given,
And perish by the hangman's rope in 1707.'

A strange coincidence – in 1707, a descendant of this Symonds, together with his mother-in-law Palmer and two other desperate villains, murdered a Mrs Palmer at Upton Snodsbury, she being the mother of Palmer, and set fire to her house; afterwards they were all executed at Worcester and afterwards gibbeted. The manor of White Lady's Aston then reverted to Bishop Lloyd, who forfeited it because it was blood money and founded a charity for the education of forty boys and about the same number of girls, at Worcester, called Bishop Lloyd's charity. The old Court, which contained fifty-two large rooms and 365 doors and windows in the time of Justice Symonds, was taken down about half a century ago, and a farmhouse built on the site, now the property of W. Berkeley, Esq.

There are two tales of ghostly coaches from villages to the west of Worcester. The Court-house at Little Shelsey is haunted by the spirit of Lady Lightfoot who was imprisoned and murdered in the house. She drives up to the house, circles it, and then drives straight through it, uttering the most ghastly screams. Sometimes the entire equipage ends up in the moat where it disappears leaving the water 'smoking like a furnace'.

Likewise at Leigh Court where Richard Colles, a Justice of the Peace who used to live there during the reign of Queen Elizabeth I, would return each St Catherine's Eve. A soft tinkle of silver bells heralded his arrival and then 'Old Colles' appeared, driving a coach with eight coal-black horses. He would drive round the moated house thirteen times before vanishing over the great tithe barn and into the River Teme.

'This perturbed spirit was at length laid in a neighbouring pool by twelve parsons at twelve at night, by the light of an inch of candle; and, as he was not to rise again until the candle was quite burnt out, it was therefore thrown into the (neighbouring) pool, and to make all sure the pool was filled up.'

A beautiful account of the legends of the Malverns appeared in one of the small guides to the folklore of the West Country that were produced by the Great Western Railway in the 1920s:

Near the middle of England, where the Malvern Hills rise abruptly to a height of nearly 1,400 feet above the sea, is the double-peaked rugged Raggedstone hill about which several strange old legends centre. A restless spirit is said to haunt the bleaker portions of the summit, but a stranger legend is that of the Shadow Curse, called down upon this hill by a monk of Little Malvern in the olden time.

Little Malvern lies in the plain at the foot of these hills, and at the Benedictine monastery there, as the old story tells, there was once a rebellious brother. His offences against the monastic discipline were so serious that the Prior decreed, as his punishment, that he should crawl on hands and knees every day and in all weather, for a certain period, from the monastery to the top of the Raggedstone and back again.

The wretched monk had to obey, and day after day, week after week, he performed his penance. But the pain and degradation of his task embittered him, and they say that before his punishment was completed he died upon the hill of exhaustion and humiliation. Others say that he sold his soul to the devil in order to be free of his hated task, but anyhow before he disappeared from human ken, he put a bitter curse upon the hill that had caused him so much suffering.

He cursed with death or misfortune whomsoever the shadow of the hill should fall upon, having in mind that in those days of sparsely populated land the people who would suffer most would be the Prior and his brethren in the monastery beneath.

Now the shadow of the Raggedstone is very seldom seen. Only at rare times when the sun is shining between the twin peaks does it appear, and those who have seen it describe it as a weird cloud, black and columnar in shape, which rises up between the two summits and moves slowly across the valley.

Many stories were told, in times past, of the misfortunes that happened to those upon whom this uncanny shadow fell; and it is recorded that Cardinal Wolsey was once caught by this weird cloud, and to that the old folk attribute the misfortune that came to the proud man when at the height of his power.

Gloucester and the South-West

Gloucester Cathedral

Gloucester and the South-West

Kenulph, King of Mercia, founded Winchcombe Abbey in 798: by the time of his death in 821 it was one of the most prosperous foundations in England and already had a complement of more than 300 Benedictine monks.

When he died Kenulph left his son Kenelm, then only seven years of age, in the charge of his elder sister Quendrida. An evil and ambitious woman, she bribed a tutor to murder Kenelm and he was taken on a hunting expedition to Clenth Wood where he was killed and buried. The version of the story related in *The Winchcombe and Sudely Record* of June 1894 continues:

This villainy, so secretly committed in England, was miraculously revealed in Rome by a white dove that dropped a parchment on St Peter's. On this evidence great multitudes assembled – a pillar of light appeared over the grave of Kenelm to which they were guided by a white cow which used to frequent the valley which afterwards became known as The Valley of the White Cow.

Kenelm's wicked sister knew nothing of this miraculous revelation. When she was confronted by the angry crowd that had come to her hotfoot from the newly discovered grave she was singing from a psalter that she held in her hands. Divine vengeance tore her eyes from their sockets and scattered blood on the verse 'This is the work of them who defame me to the Lord, and who speak evil against my soul' (Psalm 107). Both Gloucester and Worcester tried to acquire Kenelm's remains as holy relics but the Abbot of Winchcombe prevailed and erected a shrine to hold them that was much visited and saw many miracles.

In 1091 lightning struck the tower of the Abbey and toppled the crucifix and a statue of Our Lady. The church was filled with

... a stench so noisome as to be insufferable to human nostrils. At length the monks with auspicious boldness, entering, defeated the contrivances of the devil by the spilling of holy water.

The Abbey was subsequently rebuilt but was completely razed by Henry VIII. Two stone coffins that were said to have contained the bodies of Kenulph and his son may be seen in Winchcombe church. The site of the Abbey is said to sound with the chants and hymns of a ghostly choir at midnight, while near the old railway station to the north of the village a dark apparition, most like a monk in a cassock, walks two feet above ground level. Another phantom monk appears at Pyke Bank, while Margrett's Hollow has been the scene of a strange manifestation which caused a cyclist to believe his machine to be enchanted. It became impossible to ride although he could find no fault with it and eventually he had to give up and drag it ignominiously along the road.

Two miles to the north-east of Winchcombe are the remains of Hailes Abbey – a once-prosperous Cistercian foundation of the thirteenth century. This was famous for its phial that was supposed to contain drops of the Holy Blood, which attracted many pilgrims. In Hailes Church the parish register records entries from 1570. One of them reads:

Hailes Abbey

The gret plag 1603. In it 50 did, and 50 ravens flew about the steeple till all the 50 was ded. A gret wonder to see it. A gret wonder indee.

Local folk-lore believes that if a rook settles on a town house illness or death will follow. Likewise bad luck will be the result if one sees a solitary rook flying.

A disparaging account of ghosts comes from the *Tewkesbury Yearly Register & Magazine*, 1836:

JUNE:– For several weeks, about this period, some idle vagabond, dressed in various hideous garbs, occasionally secreted himself in the plantations which run parallel with the lane leading to the Lower Lode Ferry, with the foolish intention of frightening the passers-by. He generally selected the evening 'for playing the ghost'; and his usual

plan was, when he saw females approaching, to leave his
lurking-place, suddenly start into the road, and keeping at
a proper distance, endeavour by strange and ludicrous
gestures to terrify them: before his victims reached either
end of the lane, where they might have an opportunity of
giving an alarm or if a man accidentally came in sight, the
ghost, as Shakespeare says,
Started like a guilty thing
Upon a fearful summons.
Several women from the country were seriously
frightened, and for some time few females could be found
sufficiently courageous to pass the road alone. The current
belief was, that the ghost of a man who, it was said, had
many years before been murdered there, regularly paid a
nocturnal visit to the scene of his horrid death. If,
however, 'the spirits of the dead may walk again', there
was no authority for imagining that any murder had ever
been committed in that vicinity. Several men at length
determined to lie in wait and entrap the pretended ghost;
but it would appear that he became apprised of their
intention and by abandoning his wicked and dangerous
freaks, escaped the summary punishment and exposure
which he justly deserved.

The sceptic might reply that ghosts too very rarely appear when
people go looking for them.

In his *Gazetteer of British Ghosts* Peter Underwood tells of
finding another ghost resident in Cheltenham – though he fails to
reveal its address, only that it haunted a 'large house formerly a
school and now divided into flats'. This description would also fit
the house that was once the home of Imogen Swinhoe (see 'The
Cheltenham Ghost' page 58).

In this case the figure is clearly defined as a nun in a white
habit. In 1939 and in 1940 she appeared at precisely six-fifteen in
the evening on the last day of the year, on the latter occasion to a
couple of people who laid in wait for her (which belies my remarks
above about hunting for ghosts, though I believe this to be true
generally). Since 1940 there have been no reports of this ghost
reappearing.

One of the ghosts of Gloucester has a particularly unnerving trait – an unseen hand helps a visitor on with his coat in the Bishop's House. A hooded monk used to haunt 120 Westgate Street but he has not been heard of since this building was pulled down. Cats would never go into the room at the back of the house frequented by the ghost. Likewise there was a room above an archway by St Mary's which terrified dogs. This room gave a grandstand view of the burning of Bishop Hooper on 9 February 1555. He had been accused of heresy by Queen Mary.

Stories about the city's ghosts were encouraged by a particularly steely-nerved band of 'Resurrection Men' at the time when premiums were paid for corpses for use in medical teaching or research. No questions were asked of the unsavoury ruffians as to how they actually came by the bodies, but it was common knowledge that newly closed graves were often raided for their contents. At Gloucester the ghoulish raiders invented several ghosts and put the fear of the Devil into innocent passers-by just to discourage people from investigating strange lights and noises emanating from cemeteries. Once they were discovered in an open grave playing cards on the lid of a coffin.

The following account of the ghost of Archdeacon Street School was sent to us by Bob Jenkins of Longlevens, Gloucester. We are very grateful to him for allowing us to print it here:

Archdeacon Street School was for years the local school for the Westgate area of Gloucester until in the re-organisation of local government around 1968 it was decided that it should be given a facelift and used as a school for the mentally sub-normal.

During the decorating the workmen used the headmaster's office, a small room under a flight of stone steps, as a store for their paint and ladders. On a few occasions they returned in the morning to find everything moved about – tins of paint spilt and heaped in a muddle on the floor. Vandals could be ruled out as the door was still firmly locked and the one small window barred.

The caretaker, Mrs Westwood, has had strange feelings about someone following her through the building during her evening rounds. Once when she was in the boiler room she heard steps on the stairs and, thinking that it was the cleaner, asked her to pass the shovel. Instead the shovel hit her, its handle striking her face, yet there was no one to be seen.

Previously she had not been afraid of the ghost as she thought that it might be the spirit of her late husband trying to contact her; after this she was unable to enter the premises alone. The police frequently called her out in the middle of the night when they found every light in the place had been turned on.

When the school was again occupied, the children told the teachers that they had seen an old man with white hair wearing a gown and mortar-board in the manner of teachers of the nineteenth century. He was most often seen on the stairs at the top landing. He was never seen by grown-ups but only by these mentally sub-normal children who said that he seemed friendly and smiled as he watched them at their classes. They called him Charlie.

With the help of a contact on the local paper I arranged to spend Midsummer Night's Eve at the school with a couple of friends. We held a seance to speak with the ghost of the schoolteacher. We soon made contact with him and he told us that he taught at the school long ago and had accidentally fallen down the stone steps outside the headmaster's office. He had died soon afterwards on the couch in the office. We asked him if there was anything we could do for him, but he replied that he thought not. He said that he had spent his life at the school and had been very happy there. The alterations had upset him which is why he had spilt the paint. He had not wanted to harm Mrs Westwood but was simply trying to help her.

I gather that his death had been so sudden that he was unable to accept it and still thought of the school as being his. It is now an annexe of the local College of Technology; I expect the classes still have an invisible watcher.

In December 1979 the *Gloucester Citizen* carried reports of strange happenings that occurred during the demolition of a Victorian hospital – Gambier Parry Lodge in Tewkesbury Road.

Once the building was a children's hospital run by an order of nuns and there is a story of a young nun hanging herself in the building after the death of a baby in her care. When this part of the building was subsequently used as a nurses' home the figure of a nun carrying a baby was seen by several people. The crying of a baby was also frequently heard even though there were no infants in the building. However, all who saw or heard the ghost agreed on its being a benevolent presence, though the demolition men had doubts about this and preferred to work in pairs, specially when working in the chapel, morgue, and the corridor where the ghost had most often been seen. They were upset by the feeling of an invisible something standing behind them, but found that as the demolition-work progressed, so the effect of the strange presence diminished. The site will possibly be used for a housing development.

To the west of Gloucester on the banks of the Severn is the remote village of Arlingham. On 24 May 1757 the occupants of the Court House looked out of the windows and saw a ghostly funeral making its way up the grand avenue approach to the mansion. When they rushed out of doors to investigate further the cortège

Near Uley, Gloucestershire

had vanished. Twelve months later to the day the last male heir to the property, John Yate, died.

The steep, densely wooded valleys around Nailsworth and Stroud, with their multiplicity of narrow lanes, would seem to be ideal haunts for the denizens of darkness. A ghostly white figure haunts the steepest part of the lane that climbs from Nailsworth to Box. He is usually seen sitting quietly on a bench by the roadside. A similar figure is to be encountered in the dark lane that leads from the Weighbridge Inn, Avening, to Minchinhampton. It is supposed to appear at the place where a member of the Playne family was murdered or took his own life about 180 years ago. At Leonard Stanley there is a hooded monk that haunts the churchyard, and at Uley the body of a murdered Scottish pedlar was laid in the church porch for three Sundays in the belief that if the man that killed him came by the corpse would bleed.

Owlpen Manor, close to Uley, is reputed to be much haunted. During the last war the owner, an American lady, was asked to look after a small group of young refugees from one of Britain's industrial cities. When she saw them at breakfast on the day after their arrival she was asked why she wasn't wearing the lovely clothes that she had had on the previous evening. She was very puzzled by this as she had not seen the children then, and on asking for a fuller description realised that they had met a lady dressed in the fashion of four hundred or so years ago. Traditionally the house is supposed to be haunted by the restless spirit of Margaret of Anjou who stayed here before the Battle of Tewkesbury in 1471, after which she was imprisoned and her son, Prince Edward, killed.

In the *Gentleman's Magazine*, 1766, William Dallaway, High Sheriff of Gloucestershire, wrote of the sad fate of a local young squire who uttered one profanity too many:

On February 20 last, Richard Parsons and three more met at a private house in Chalford, in order to play at cards, about six o' clock in the evening. They played at loo till about eleven or twelve at night, when they changed their game for whist. After a few deals a dispute arose about the state of the game. Parsons asserted, with oaths, that they were six, which the others denied: upon which he wished 'that he might never enter into the Kingdom of Heaven, and that his flesh might rot upon his bones, if there were not six in the game'. These wishes were several times repeated, both then and afterwards. Presently they adjourned to another house, and there began a fresh game, when Parsons and his partner had great success. Then they played at loo again till four in the morning. During the second playing, Parsons complained to one Rolles, his partner, of a bad pain in his leg, which from that time increased. There was an appearance of a swelling, and afterwards the colour changed to that of a mortified state. On the following Sunday he rode to Minchinhampton, to get the advice of Mr Pegler, the surgeon in that town, who attended him on the Thursday after February 27. Notwithstanding all the applications that were made, the mortification increased and showed itself in different parts of the body. On Monday March 3 at the request of some of his female relations the clergyman of Bisley attended him and administered the Sacrament without any knowledge of what had happened before, and which he continued a stranger to till he saw the account in the *Gloucester Journal*. Parsons appeared to be extremely ignorant of religion, having been accustomed to swear, to drink (though he was not in liquor when he uttered the above execrable wish), to game, and profane the Sabbath, though he was only in his 19th year; yet, after he had received the Sacrament, he appeared to have some sense of the ordinance; for he said 'Now must I never sin again'; he hoped God would forgive him, having been wicked not above six years, and that whatever should happen, he would not play at cards again.

After this he was in great agony, chiefly delirious, spoke of his companions by name and seemed as if his imagination was engaged at cards. He started, had distracted looks and gestures, and in a dreadful fit of shaking and trembling, died on Tuesday morning, the 4th of March last, and was buried the next day at the parish church at Bisley. His eyes were open when he died, and could not be closed by the ordinary methods; so they remained open when he was put in the coffin. From this circumstance arose a report, that he wished his eyes might never close; but this was a mistake; for, from the most creditable witnesses, I am fully convinced no such wish was uttered; and the fact is, that he did close his eyes after he was taken with the mortification and either dosed or slept several times. When the body came to be laid out, it appeared all over discoloured or spotted: and it might, in the most literal sense, be said that his flesh rotted on his bones before he died. It is to be hoped that his sad catastrophe will serve to admonish all those who profane the sacred name of God.

This instant retribution must have made many a hard-drinking countryman have second thoughts on his way of life. Less relevant to our subject but slightly more edifying is the next story which comes from *Gloucestershire Extracts*, 1876:

A Curious Custom – The observance of a curious custom in a country village led to magisterial proceedings at Whitminster on Thursday last. The good folks of Randwick, a village about two miles from Stroud, have a custom by which on the 9th April they elect a 'Mayor' for the year ensuing, and the election generally gives rise to some disorderly proceedings. One method of celebrating the event is to 'duck' somebody in the village pond, and it was the selection of an unwilling and resisting person for this purpose that led to an assault. The aggrieved party, however, declined to prosecute, and the defender got off by paying the costs. So far as we have been able to learn, the only 'privilege' which his worship possesses is that when he finds three pigs sleeping together he may turn one of them out and himself sleep between the other two!

A recurring supernatural 'wonder' was the door, table, or floor which would run with blood on a certain day, usually the anniversary of a murder. On St Matthew's Day, 1646, such an occurrence took place at Baunton:

There rose out of an old day table bord of birch . . . a water, reddish of the colour of blood, and so continued till

125

rising and runninge alonge and downe the table, all that afternoone and the nighte following till the next day. . . .

Modern science can explain that most probably the phenomenon is due to the bacteria *Serratia marcescens*, which has played a notable role in history. It may well have been responsible for turning up, like drops of blood, in the bread of the soldiers of Alexander the Great besieging Tyre in 332 B C. Inspired by this omen they were revitalised and took the city. In Christian times the appearance of a blood-like substance in broken bread has been taken as a sign of divine approval, a moment graphically captured by Raphael in his masterpiece *The Mass at Bolsena*, in which a doubting priest has his faith renewed when drops of blood are seen on the bread offered at the Eucharist. In this century this microbe has been extensively used as a marker in bacteriological experiments. Because of this it has grown increasingly resistant to antibiotics and is the cause of serious epidemics in hospitals (*The Guardian*, 20 December 1979).

Science has little to do with the various methods of laying ghosts. One peculiar to the area appears to have been in use around Northleach. The essential ingredients were a barrel of spirits and twelve priests, though as, if the exorcism was successful, one of the latter would die within the year, the difficulty was in persuading the clergy to take part. After the ceremony the barrel of spirits was left in a room of the house that was seldom used. Then masons and carpenters were called in to seal the chamber off completely so that no hint remained of its existence, even the windows having been bricked up. Shipton Court and Lodge Park (between Northleach and Aldsworth) are two local houses said to possess 'vanished' rooms.

Cirencester is a town of beautiful old buildings, and typical of them is the rambling Black Horse Inn, which claims to be the town's oldest pub, dating from the fifteenth century. It was the scene of remarkable supernatural events in 1933, beginning on 13 August when Ruby Bower, the niece of the licensee, woke up at midnight aware of a subtle alteration in the atmosphere of the room in which she slept. When she opened her eyes she found it bathed in a weird light and her worst fears were realised when she heard a gentle rustling sound from one of the corners of the room.

Looking in this direction she was horrified to see 'an apparition in the shape of a stout old lady with an evil face and grim expression, gliding slowly across the floor. Despite her fears, and the fact that the whole thing could not have lasted more than a fraction of a second, every detail is indelibly impressed on Miss Bower's memory. She recalls the old-fashioned clothes of the midnight visitor, the long fawn-coloured dress of a stiff silk that rustled as the old lady moved, the white apron with its frills, and the white frilly mob cap.'

The poor girl naturally screamed out loudly whereupon the ghost walked out through the opposite wall of the room. Strangely, the room had been newly altered, and panelling shut it off from the outside wall and the windows, but Ruby told her uncle that she distinctly remembered seeing windows in the room. When the room was searched nothing unusual was found until they looked on the far side of the new panelling. There, newly scratched into the glass of a window-pane, was the name 'James' written several times in an ornate old-fashioned script.

The local newspaper, *The Vale of White Horse Gazette* (whose contemporary account is quoted above), made a great thing of this story, and in a 'follow-up' sought out the help of an anonymous lady endowed with psychic powers to solve the mystery.

She was taken to the inn knowing nothing of the circumstances of the haunting. On entering she told the landlord of changes to the building that had taken place many years before, that only he knew of. She refused to enter one room on the ground floor, and made the same reaction to the rooms situated immediately above on the two upper floors. As she went into one of the bedrooms a remarkable change occurred to her physique. She seemed to age suddenly, her frame twisted to reflect arthritic suffering, and her voice became that of an old woman. She limped through a succession of further rooms, whispering to her awestruck companions that she felt the burden of a great sadness as well as the stiffness and pain of old age.

When she came to the haunted room she resumed her normal posture and her voice regained its strength. She told Ruby and her uncle that there was nothing to fear. 'There was an old man

Ghostly writing on a window-pane. Upside-down, the name 'James' is clearly revealed

and an old lady. The old lady has a long chin and a long beak-like nose. She is earth-bound, she has done the old man some injury and wanders about the house. But the harm she would do or has done is not in this room. It is in one of the rooms I would not enter.'

Later the medium gave instructions on how to lay the ghost. At 3 p.m. on the third day of the month three white flowers had to be laid in Room 3. This was not the scene of the haunting but the room which the clairvoyant refused to enter. It had then to be left unopened for three days. This appears to have been successful, and though in *Haunted Inns* Marc Alexander quotes a modern landlord as saying that there have been a number of further strange occurrences the present landlord has heard of no recent activity.

An earlier apparition at Cirencester is mentioned in John Aubrey's *Miscellanies*, 1670. The person to whom it appeared asked it whether it were a good spirit or bad, on which it disappeared 'with a curious perfume and most melodious twang. Mr W. Lilley believes it was a fairy.'

Perhaps Aubrey's ghost was the one that still appears at the King's Head, the famous old hotel in the Market Place. A ghost there has been responsible for disturbing the peace of mind of a succession of night porters, though it seems to have met its match in the present one, Mr Charles Anderson, who is a man well-used to ghosts. One haunted a house in which he used to live in Gloucester Street that was formerly an old smithy. Here the door would open and close of its own accord and the smell typical of a smithy, of hot iron and burning hoof, would flood into the room. However, the ghost was always friendly and when Charles' grown-up daughter was left alone in the house when the rest of the family were on holiday he would accompany her upstairs each night, leaving her at the bedroom door.

Thus, when Charles took on the job at the King's Head, he was not disturbed when told of the presence of a ghost in the building. He was certainly determined not to be intimidated by it as the previous night porters had been – the management had difficulty in keeping men in this post for any length of time. Within a few nights Mr Anderson was made aware of the presence of the ghost.

He saw a dim figure standing on the stairs early one morning and thinking it a guest asked if it were feeling all right. When no answer was forthcoming he looked closer and saw that it was wearing a monk's robe with the cowl drawn up around the face, but this was invisible. The apparition disappeared suddenly through the wall.

Since that occasion Charles has had many encounters with the ghost, though he has only seen it on one further occasion. This was when one of the barmaids asked if she could accompany him on his rounds to see the parts of the old building that few people knew. When they came to the Monks' Retreat – the undercroft of the hotel now used as a skittle alley and party-room – Charles opened the door for her and paused while he waited for her to enter. Instead she gave a loud scream, pointing at the dark faceless figure that was seated on a stool by the entrance. As she screamed the figure slowly vanished, yet the stool continued to rock gently. After this the barmaid left the hotel, returning to her parents in the North of England, and she was so upset by the incident that she was unable to work for some time afterwards.

Although these are the only two occasions when the ghost has actually been seen by Mr Anderson it has frequently made its presence known in other ways. He is quite accustomed to a firm grip being placed on his shoulder in the middle of the night. This, he admits, would be unnerving to a person less used to ghosts but he has an infallible way of making the unwelcome presence stop its mischief – 'I just tell him to b– off in no uncertain tone and then he's as good as gold.' He believes that though the spirit is playful it is seldom malevolent and he almost enjoys its unseen presence as otherwise the routine of the long night would be even more tedious.

'He can get up to all sorts of tricks,' he told me, 'and often he shakes the plastic curtains that are drawn down over the cocktail bar – yet all the windows are shut and so there's no draught to stir them. Then again he moves the heavy electric fire in the hallway; he really makes that dance about and it's made of cast iron. Another time he set the old Symphonion going by the entrance doors, but that only works when someone puts an old penny in the slot. The front door often opens of its own accord when the outer

Charles Anderson in the Monk's Retreat

door is bolted tight, and I can always tell when he's about by this icy draught up the back of my neck.'

Even guests have been disturbed by the ghost. On a couple of occasions they have been terrified to find themselves held firmly down to the bed by a strange force. One visitor came trembling downstairs and told Charles of his experience. 'He was almost relieved to be told that it was only a favourite antic of the ghost, but he said his arms and legs were aching like hell after his struggle to get off the bed. After a cup of tea he returned to his room quite happily.'

The week before my visit to the hotel, early in 1980, Charles had heard mysterious footsteps coming from the front bedrooms in the old part of the building. He knew that these rooms were all unoccupied as they were being redecorated, and on checking found them all locked and empty. He returned downstairs but continued to hear the footsteps throughout the night.

Other members of the staff have also had encounters with the supernatural. A poltergeist has flung a pen across the Whitelock Suite putting the fear of God into a porter who was alone in the room at the time. A fireball (perhaps caused by static electricity) danced across the ballroom before smashing itself against one of the mirrors. Both a chambermaid and a relief porter have seen a ghostly cavalier. This ghost scared both unfortunate witnesses with its appearance, especially in the latter instance when it fired an old-fashioned pistol at the porter, who abruptly left the job the next day. This haunting may well be a re-enactment of a dramatic incident which took place at the King's Head in 1688 (and wonderfully shown in the oil painting in the upstair cocktail bar). Lord Lovelace, who was on his way to join the forces of William of Orange, was attacked by a party of Stuart supporters under Captain Lorange in the Market Place. During this affray a companion of Lord Lovelace, Bulstrode Whitelock, was shot and died in the King's Head.

In the Monks' Retreat is the entry of a blocked-up passageway which once led underneath the Market Place to the cellars of the Abbey Penitentiary – hence the name given to the undercroft today.

The Centre and the South

The Langston Arms Hotel

The Centre and the South

Stow-on-the-Wold is situated at the very heart of the Cotswolds – a hilltop town where eight roads converge, the most important being the Fosse Way. An unassuming semi-detached house in Chapen Street was plagued by a particularly unpleasant poltergeist during 1963–4. Mysterious pools of water appeared throughout the house, and although officials from the council and water board made intensive searches, no cause for this could be found. Furniture was moved about and the fourteen-year-old son of this house tipped out of bed. The violence steadily increased: sheets were ripped in two and deep gouge-marks were found in the headboard of a bed. Strange writing appeared on walls where wallpaper had been ripped off. A baby's hand was seen that steadily grew into the fist of a fully grown man. Finally a voice was heard that explained that these sinister and disturbing incidents were caused by one of the builders of the house who had died twenty years before. A check was made, and sure enough the haunting had begun on the anniversary of this man's death – 15 February. Even when the family went away on holiday they were unable to escape the attention of the poltergeist, though eventually it seems that they were able to accept its activities and live with it in a reasonably normal way.

The year 1964 seems to have been a good one for ghosts in this locality. The Langston Arms Hotel at Kingham had the reputation of being haunted before then, but in that year the ghost was particularly active, appearing to the landlord or the customers every ten days or so in the form of a white shape that resembled the figure of a nun in a head-dress. Shuffling footsteps and other strange sounds, rather like someone coughing, often announced the appearance of the ghost. Room No. 1 seems to be most favoured by this presence: dogs will refuse to enter and their hair stands on end if they are taken anywhere near it. Although the building is only about 200 years old, its foundations are said to be much more ancient, and there is a story of a bricked-up secret passageway that led to Bruern Abbey. Some years ago an attempt was made to exorcise the ghost by the then vicar of Rissington; apparently it was unsuccessful.

Another tunnel is supposed to link Tangley Hall with the Abbey, four miles away. It is probably a monk from this foundation who haunts the lonely footpath that leads from Milton-under-Wychwood to Fifield.

A 'little brown monk' haunts the ancient Priory at Burford, which has been the retreat of a sisterhood of Roman Catholic nuns since 1947. Before this the Priory was a private house, described as 'very haunted', and an owner believed that it would stay this way until the building was returned to the Church. However, strange sounds are still heard: a bell rings mysteriously at two in the morning – the time when medieval monks were awoken for their night-time devotions – and the singing of a choir is heard. The little brown monk has been seen by the nuns in the Chapel and elsewhere in the Priory. The Old Rectory also belongs to the convent (it is the Chaplain's residence). Its ghost is less tranquil than that of the monk and hurls articles around a disused room. There is an 'overwhelming atmosphere of sadness' about the house. The grounds are frequented by the stern figure of a gamekeeper who carries a blunderbuss and walks through any object that stands in his way.

The road between Burford and Minster Lovell is feared for its strange black cloud which, if it envelops you, generates an overpowering feeling of terror. If animals are caught in it they are driven frantic and some never recover.

Minster Lovell Hall is haunted by the spirit of Lord Lovell who disastrously chose to support the cause of the pretender, Lambert Simnel, in 1487. After the Battle of Stoke in which the rebellion was quashed he hid in a secret room in the Hall, looked after by one servant who was the only person who knew his whereabouts. Unfortunately this servant died and the hiding-place remained secret until 1718 when it was revealed by structural alterations. Lord Lovell's skeleton was seated at the table; at his feet were the bones of his dog.

Burford Priory

Close to the airbase at Brize Norton is the tiny village of Lew. The Manor Farm here is reputed to be haunted. The ghost seems to enjoy appearing to the wives of American airmen who often stay at the house. The bells outside the doors of the bedrooms ring for no obvious reason and dogs seem to dislike going upstairs.

Many strange stories have been told about Cowleas Corner, on the road between Bampton and Clanfield. Long, long ago suicides were buried here 'at dead of night and by torchlight'. There was also a belief that a treasure was buried in the bank of the road at this spot, and even at the end of the last century old people would dig trenches in attempts to find the hoard. A catalogue of weird happenings which have occurred here would include:

– A rolling object like a wool-pack, which travelled a vast distance across the countryside passing through a multitude of obstacles before vanishing into the fish-pond near the Lady Well at Ham Court (also known as the Manor House, presumably at Bampton, see below).

– A naked man who appeared when a shepherd looked over his shoulder for his dog and then just as suddenly vanished.

– A variety of beast-like shapes and the figure of an old man 'dressed in a low-crowned hat and a light-coloured foul-weather great-coat, such as the shepherds of the neighbourhood are known to wear'. This was pursued by the observer, but was easily able to maintain the same distance until it passed into a field by the Manor House and took the shape of a calf.

– Something like a flash of lightning accompanied by a clap of thunder. The ghost 'glided backwards and forwards with the speed of light and the intangibility of a vapour, through the cart of the astonished higler, as if he would cut it to pieces. It is not surprising that the horse, frightened at these doings, took to its heels. . . .'

It would seem that none of these stories would convince an angry wife when her husband turned up late from market smelling strongly of drink.

The Manor House at Bampton may still contain the spirit of a ghost that was layed in a barrel of strong beer and then walled-up in a cellar: it was still there in 1894. This is the earth-bound soul of a Mrs Whittaker whose husband fell in love with a maidservant in the town. His wife died of a broken heart and her ghost returned to haunt the place. It was laid eventually in a nearby pond but when this dried up, 'so strong' was her ghost that the service had to be gone through again, and this time the spirit secured in the cask of strong beer.

A ghost named Horace haunts the Talbot Hotel at Bampton. He was written up in the *Witney Gazette* in November, 1973, and appears to be the ghost of one of the staff who lived in a small, well-concealed room at the top of the hotel during the 1950s.

Another unwelcome guest at a hotel is Mad Maude who haunts the Weston Manor Hotel at Weston-on-the-Green. The building was once a monastery and Maude a nun who made clandestine visits to one of the monks from her convent nearby. One night she was caught in her lover's cell, brought to trial, and burnt at the stake in front of the monastery. Nothing is known of the fate of the monk, or the reason for the nun being called 'Mad', unless she was a somewhat slow-witted girl who was enticed to the place by lecherous monks. She is said to return to the scene of her trysts,

Weston Manor

J.C.Buckler.del.1811. Part of STANTON HARCOURT HOUSE, called POPE'S TOWER, with the CHURCH, Oxfordshire. *B.Holler sculp.*

and of her subsequent agonising death, particularly to the best bedroom of the hotel which contains a fine four-poster bed.

The obsession of folk in this part of the Cotswolds with laying ghosts in ponds turns up again in two stories of Stanton Harcourt. Pope stayed at Stanton Harcourt in 1718 and composed much of his *Odyssey* there. The room he used is in the tower that still bears his name. Lady Alice Harcourt was murdered in this tower while other members of the family were at Mass. She was cut to pieces and thrown out of one of the small windows. Her spirit haunted the grounds until it was laid in one of the ponds (and Pope wrote of this incident in a letter sent during his visit). Another ghost was laid in these ponds – the spirit of a lady who drowned herself. She reappears when the pond dries out, often in a coach and four.

At the Manor Farm the ghost of a Mrs Hall used to haunt the house and the garden of the nearby inn, the Harcourt Arms. She poisoned herself when she found that her husband was seeing the landlady 'after hours'. She too was eventually laid in a pond, though again the ghost will return should the pond ever dry up.

Bibliography

Much of the material came from nineteenth-century scrapbooks at Birmingham, Gloucester, and Stratford-upon-Avon public libraries.

Other sources include:

Warwickshire & Worcestershire Life, December 1971
The Folklore of Shakespeare's Land by J. Harvey Bloom (London 1929)
Oxford and Country Ghost Stories by John Richardson
The Folklore of the Cotswolds by Katharine M. Briggs (London 1974)
Witney Gazette, 22 November 1973
Country Life, 11 July 1963
The Cheltenham Ghost by B. Adby Collins (London 1948)
The Campden Wonder by Sir George Clark (Oxford 1959)
Murder by Witchcraft by Donald McCormick (London 1968)
The Gloucester Citizen, 27 December 1954
Hauntings by Peter Underwood (London 1977)
The Stroud Journal, 21 September 1951
Notes & Queries (various volumes)
Gentleman's Magazine, 1794, etc.
Winchcombe Record, November 1892, June 1894
Tewkesbury Yearly Register & Magazine, 1836
Gloucestershire Extracts, 1876
Shakespeare's Greenwood by G. Morley
The Folklore of Warwickshire by Roy Palmer
Birmingham Weekly Post, 26 August 1905
Ackermann's 'Repository', November 1820
Highways & Byways in Oxford and the Cotswolds by C. Griggs
Stories and Legends of the Cotswolds by Stanley Jackson-Coleman (Isle of Man 1961)
Stratford-upon-Avon Herald, 23 February 1945
Haunted Inns by Marc Alexander
The Bromsgrove Messenger, 27 March 1909
The Weekly Post (various issues)
The Evesham Journal (various issues)
Witchcraft and Demonianism by C. L'Estrange Ewen (London 1933)
The Natural History of the Vampire by Anthony Masters
Focus (various issues)
Gazetteer of British Ghosts by Peter Underwood

Index

Acknowledgments

The illustrations came from a wide variety of sources and we are indebted to the following for allowing us to use their material:

Ashmolean Museum, Oxford (pages 18, 66, 78, 87, 89, 97, 99, 103, 139).

Cambridge University Library (pages 6, 106, 142).

The British Library (pages 39, 47).

The *Stratford-upon-Avon Herald* (page 53).

The National Portrait Gallery (page 110).

The remainder of the material was supplied from the Photographic Library of Jarrold Publishing, for whom Tim Hunt drew the sketches that appear on pages 30, 49, 51 and 118.